Charles Hedley

The Atoll of Funafuti, Ellice Group

Its zoology, botany, ethnology, and general structure based on collections made by

Mrs. Charles Hedley, of the Australian museum, Sydney, N. S. W

Charles Hedley

The Atoll of Funafuti, Ellice Group

Its zoology, botany, ethnology, and general structure based on collections made by Mrs. Charles Hedley, of the Australian museum, Sydney, N. S. W

ISBN/EAN: 9783337315368

Printed in Europe, USA, Canada, Australia, Japan

Cover: Foto ©Andreas Hilbeck / pixelio.de

More available books at **www.hansebooks.com**

THE MOLLUSCA.

Part I. — Gasteropoda.

By CHARLES HEDLEY.

Many of the introductory remarks which prefaced collections previously dealt with, apply with equal force to the Mollusca. Little was known of the Mollusca of the Ellice Group prior to our Expedition. With one exception, none of the naturalists—Dana, Whitmee, Woodford, Finsch—who have been to the archipelago, gathered any shells. The exception being Dr. Ed. Graeffe, who visited most of the atolls in the interest of the Godeffroy Museum. The land shells he procured are described by Mousson.* A few other animals described by German authors from this group were probably also collected by him.

The poverty of the fauna of the atoll, compared with that of any continental area lying under corresponding latitudes, such as Queensland, New Guinea, or the Melanesian Plateau, again asserts itself. Whole groups, the Brachiopoda and the Polyplacophora, are missing, giving to the fauna an unsymmetrical aspect. Especially significant is the absence of Mollusca with large eggs such as *Nautilus, Melo,* or *Voluta* from this drifted fauna. In many cases the Funafuti shells are smaller than the usual stature of their respective species. Harper Pease has remarked that the marine Gasteropoda of the Paumotus are in general dwarfed in comparison with those of Tahiti.† Shipley mentions that specimens of Gephyrean worms from Funafuti were considerably smaller than representatives of the same species from Rotuma.‡

Poor though this fauna be, I have to apologise for the following inadequate account of it. Thorough search would probably result in multiplying the known total three or four times. My commission embraced the study of the Atoll as a whole. Although the Mollusca alone would have afforded occupation for the entire time of an investigator, yet Ethnology, and Botany, and other branches of Zoology equally claimed my attention. On my return the mass of material, molluscan and otherwise, together with the

---

* Mousson—Journ. de Conch. xxi. 1873, pp. 102 - 109.
† Pease—Am. Journ. Conch. iv. 1868, p. 109.
‡ Shipley—Proc. Zool. Soc. 1898, p. 468.

pressure of current Museum duties has operated unfavourably on my report. Various inquiries on anatomy and other related matters have been perforce omitted. With the exception of a sketch of the geographical distribution I have unwillingly restricted myself to the mere systematic treatment of the species.

A superficial reader might seize on the fact that many new species are described as new in the following pages, and with a show of reason deduce that so great a proportion of novelties indicate a very peculiar and endemic fauna. This would however be a mistaken impression. Few realise how exceeding rich the fauna of the tropical Pacific is, or how poor our knowledge thereof. Probably, except in New Caledonia, a capable collector would obtain at least one shell new to science in a day's work on any beach in the South Pacific. Fischer's estimate that the Indo-Pacific Province contains five or six thousand marine mollusca,* is certainly below the mark.

For the purpose of comparison the Funafuti fauna must be divided into large conspicuous, and small inconspicuous shells. The distribution already ascertained for conspicuous genera like *Cypraea* will be paralleled, as knowledge increases, for inconspicuous genera like *Caecum*. Thus I anticipate the discovery in the western continental islands of every minute species I have described as new from Funafuti. The range of all the species mentioned is given for the South Pacific as completely as opportunity permitted. A discussion of the data collected is postponed to the concluding pages of this Memoir.

The study of the mollusca of the Pacific is attended with peculiar difficulty. As a result of the superior energy of the British in exploration, commerce and missionary enterprise in the Pacific, the vast majority of the mollusca of this region have, from the time of Captain Cook to the present day, been first examined in London. The writers who have dealt with them, Adams Bros., Hinds, Reeve, the Sowerbys, Smith, Melvill, and others, have treated them uniformly on the model and method of Lamarck ; it will be convenient to call this group of authors the " London School." A brilliant exception to the work of British writers is the superb Memoir by Boog Watson on the Gasteropoda collected by the Challenger Expedition.

As a consequence of the devotion of the London School to the study of the Pacific fauna, we have a great mass of involved synonomy, inadequate descriptions, poor figures or none, crude classification and total neglect of soft anatomy. The smaller portion of this fauna which has gone to Paris has generally been well figured, and a fraction which has fallen into the hands of

---

* Fischer—Man. de Conch. 1887, p. 157.

American students has received scientific treatment. A higher grade of work was reached by a poor, solitary, invalid exile like Montrouzier than by men who had within their reach the unrivalled resources of the collections, the libraries and artists of London.

To descend from generalities to details, it may be pointed out that whilst the foremost British and American writers in all other branches of zoology now use English ; whilst the scientific writers of other countries, like Sars and Collett in Norway, Schepman in Holland and various Japanese authors, are adopting English as an international language, on the grounds of its wide currency, wealth and flexibility ; yet this conservative London school of Conchologists reject the advantages of their mother tongue and satisfy their humble wants with the poor and awkward medium of Latin.

By some strange unwritten law these Conchologists have invariably maintained a proportion between the size of a shell and its illustration. Thus a large shell, however simple in structure, demanded a large figure ; and a small shell, however complex its details, a small drawing. Had this school encountered Pachyderms or Foraminifera, one or both would surely have fallen beyond the focus of their vision.

Though great wealth of anatomical material was profferred them, these writers have ever cast the "nasty things" aside. The fascinating studies of structure, affinities, higher classification, or geographical distribution had no charm for them. Their measure of excellence in Conchological research being apparently the highest score of new species.

But the chief defect of this school is that it has added to the superstructure without strengthening the foundation, and has thus weakened instead of improved the fabric of our knowledge. Upon the distinction of old species depends not only generic and subgeneric classification, but even the reality of new species, which are necessarily contrasted with them. The task of rehabilitating old species, for which these writers have unique facilities, is by them neglected in favour of the easier and more showy work of describing novelties, which could be done at least as well by others.

In illustration, I will cite the following case, one instance of a multitude. Hinds, in 1843,* thus described a new species, *Triforis collaris*:—"Testa ovata, acuminata ; anfractibus duodecim biseratim granulosis, serie inferiorie paululum maxima, margaritacea, superiore pallide fusca; anfractu ultimo quadriseratim subaequaliter concatenato. Axis 4 lin."

---

* Hinds—Proc. Zool. Soc., 1843, p. 23.

No one will to-day affirm that so brief an account suffices for the recognition of this species. Consequently there is every probability that it has been, or will be, again named and described to the confusion of science. In so numerous and difficult a group, a description a page long and several detailed figures are barely enough to determine a species in the absence of authentic specimens. It would be supposed that this view only required to be stated for every worker to endorse it, but for sixty-five years British writers have passed over this inadequate account and neglected to repair the fault. So recently as last year, Melvill and Standen in treating of the shells of Lifu, examined and catalogued this species, yet it never occurred to them that a figure and description was more urgently needed for *I. collaris* than for any of the hundred novelties they figured and described.

Great numbers of the species of Adams, Hinds, Smith and others are inadequately represented in literature, and cannot be recognised without an inspection of the type in London. Either therefore no Conchological work should be published except by residents of London, which is an absurd proposition, or these species must be ignored by naturalists.

The local conditions under which the Funafuti mollusca occur may be briefly sketched. The distinction between the marine and terrestrial mollusca, so sharply drawn in temperate zones, fades away in the tropics. At a distance from the sea, in close association with such forms as *Stenogyra* and *Endodonta*, occur *Littorina*, *Nerita*, *Truncatella* and *Melampus*. The outer windward beach, where the surf sweeps the narrow reef platform, is only accessible at intervals when a low tide coincides with calm weather. Here the molluscan assemblage bears the mark of incessant buffeting of waves, all are characterised by powerful muscular feet which adhere to the rock like the sucker foot of the limpet, all have thick shells mostly strengthened by knobs or ridges. In the little rock pools at the foot of the shingle beach, swarm the gaily painted shells of *Engina mendicaria*, *Mitra literata*, *Conus hebraeus* and *C. ceylonensis*. Beyond, where the surf breaks more heavily, are several species of *Sistrum*, usually nestled in a rock crevice and more or less concealed by extraneous growth upon their shells. Here also are *Purpura armigera* and *P. hippocastaneum*, and on the brink of deep water is *Turbo setosus*.

It comes as a surprise to a naturalist to find the pelagic fauna scarce in this latitude. Dr. Krämer tells me that he was greatly struck by the poverty of the tropical Pacific in this respect. One Pteropod, one Heteropod, and a fragment of *Ianthina* were all of this class that came under my notice.

The quiet waters of the lagoon prove a richer field for a collector than the storm swept ledges of the ocean beach. Just at the south end of the main islet of Funafuti, where the lagoon communicates with the ocean, are some clumps of *Millepora* rising to the surface from about ten or twelve feet. On these is a colony of the giant *Vermetus*, and built in by coral growth are *Magilus* and *Galeropsis*. Near the *Millepora* were bushes of *Plexaura*, among whose branches perched *Avicula*. A sandy flat sheltered behind a long shingle bank yielded at low water *Mitra episcopalis*, *Murex ramosus* and *Trochus obeliscus*.

A mile to the north, where the quiet waters allowed mud to settle, the gregarious *Planaxis sulcatus* occurred in quantities. *Cypraea moneta* and *C. caput serpentis* were here abundant, and to the rocks in the neighbourhood adhered *Chama*. Nearer the village, at the spot sketched on p. 71, I found as dead shells most of the small species described as new.

A few small reefs in the lagoon opposite the village were excellent collecting grounds. The sandy patches among the coral were inhabited by *Strombus luhuanus* and *S. floridus*, and by numerous Cerithidæ, among which the large *C. nodulosum* was conspicuous. What seemed a brilliantly coloured worm disappeared at a touch with a snap and proved to be the animal of *Tridacna elongata* seen through the opening of the valves sunk in coral. Loose coral blocks rolled over and split up yielded a harvest; under the block might be *Conus rattus*, *C. lividus* or *Mitra limbifera*, and within it *Lithodomus* and *Arca*.

In a few hours spent on the leeward islets of the Atoll, I gathered on the beach several large but dead species of *Cypraea*, *Oliva* and *Conus*, which I had not elsewhere encountered. A glimpse of a rich and distinct deep water fauna was afforded by a few hauls of the tangles in 80 – 40 fathoms on the western outer slope of the Atoll. Almost everything here collected appears to be new to science.

The sole representative of a fluviatile fauna was a species of *Melania* which occurred in some abundance in the native wells.

Mr. George Sweet has kindly allowed me to inspect a collection of shells he made on Funafuti in 1897. I have been able in several cases to increase my list by species which he took, but which I had not seen.

CEPHALOPODA.

I was unable to secure any specimens of Cephalopoda at Funafuti, though I observed traces of them, as beaks thrown up on the beach and ink in the hands of the natives (p 64). Pictures of an *Octopus* were recognized by the natives as "feki," and of a *Loligo* as "mofeki." I was told that on rare occasions empty *Nautilus* shells drifted to the Atoll, but the natives positively asserted that they never occurred there alive. No shells of *Spirula* were seen on the beaches.

Dr. Georg Pfeffer has described* *Loligo brevipinnis* from the Ellice Group.

No members of the BRACHIOPODA or POLYPLACOPHERA were seen in the Ellice Islands.

SCAPHOPODA.

DENTALIUM LESSONI, *Deshayes.*

Pilsbry, Man. Conch. xvii., 1898, p. 8, pl. vi., figs. 36 – 90.

Two imperfect shells found on the sandy beach of the lagoon correspond more nearly to this than to any other described form.

GASTEROPODA.

HALIOTIS STOMATIAEFORMIS, *Reeve.*

Pilsbry, Man. Conch. xii., 1890, p. 89, pl. iii., fig. 4 ; pl. xlix., figs. 30 – 35.

I found a single dead shell on the windward side of Nukulailai. Mr. Sweet has sent me specimens from Funafuti.

Pilsbry records this from New Caledonia and Fiji.

EMARGINULA CLATHRATA, *Pease.*

Pilsbry, *op. cit.*, p. 266, pl. lxiii., fig. 12; Pease, Am. Journ. Conch. iv., 1868, p. 99, pl. ii., fig. 24.

Once found alive under a stone in the lagoon. Hitherto only known from Hawaii.

EMARGINULA MARIEI, *Crosse.*

Pilsbry, *op. cit.*, p. 271, pl. xxii., figs. 34, 35, 36.

A few bleached shells were gathered on the lagoon beach.

Hitherto only known from New Caledonia.

ACMAEA SACCHARINA, *Linne.*

Pilsbry, Man. Conch. xiii., 1891, p. 49, pl. xxxvi., figs. 60, 61, 62, 78; pl. xviii., figs. 31, 32; pl. xxiv., figs. 12, 13.

A few small and dead shells inclining towards the var. *perplexa*, Pilsbry, were found on the outer beach. Schmeltz mentions it from Queensland, Samoa, and Fiji.

---

* Pfeffer, Die Cephalopoden des Hamburger Naturhistorischen Museums. —Abh. Geb. der Naturw. viii., 1884, p. 5, pl. i., fig. 4; pl. ii., fig. 4a.

PHENACOLEPAS SENTA, sp. nov.
(Fig. 1).

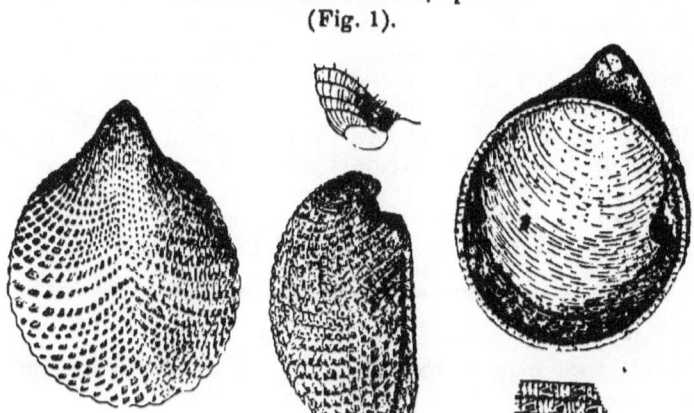

Fig. 1.

Shell cap shaped, with a protuberant and overhanging posterior apex, the earlier portion thin and translucent, the older solid and opaque ; adult shell asymmetrical by reason of a slight spiral twist. Colour white. The nepionic shell is very smooth and glossy sharply contrasting with the dull surface of the remainder, depressedly turbinate, apparently two whorled but swallowed past the nucleus by the older shell. Sculpture :—on the part next the nepionic shell there are circular growth lines, as these diverge wider their interstices are crossed by longitudinal lines which develop later into low small rounded ribs parted by slight furrows, these are reticulated by two series of fine raised threads crossing at right angles. Upon these ribs arise in quincunx order a series of V-shaped thorns, the limbs of which are directed anteriorly. A portion of the dorsal surface immediately above the posterior base is selected in the accompanying figure for illustrating this feature. Finally the limbs increase till they meet those of their neighbours and enclose a rhomboidal space, thus the marginal part of the shell becomes cancellated by a raised network, oblique both to the line of growth, the axis of the shell and the earlier sculpture. The minute transverse thread lines persist to the aperture.

Aperture subcircular, the edge when adult is broadened and finely crenulated. Interior glossy, the exterior sculpture visible through the shell. Muscular impressions are a right and left adductor scar and a narrow horse shoe marking the head line a little within the lip. Length 6, breadth $4\frac{1}{2}$, height 3 mm.

Eight empty shells from sand on the beach of Funafuti lagoon.

This species has its nearest kin in *P. cinnamomea*, Gould, but differs so widely from that by contour, sculpture and exposed nepionic shell that a new genus seems necessary to express the distinction. Yet *P. cinnamomea* itself stands perhaps as far again from the type of the genus *P. crenulata*, Broderip, and being unable to offer any information on the animal of the new species, I am unwilling to further divide a group of which our knowledge is so brief.

Scutellina of Gray (1847) being preoccupied by *Scutellina* of Agassiz (1841), Pilsbry has substituted *Phenacolepas*.*

TROCHUS OBELISCUS, *Gmelin*.

Pilsbry, Man. Conch. xi., 1889, p. 19, pl. ii., figs. 13, 14.

Several specimens were taken alive in shallow water in the lagoon associated with *Mitra episcopalis*.

Fischer quotes this from New Caledonia, Fiji, Samoa and Tonga.

TROCHUS TUBIFERUS, *Kiener*.

Pilsbry, *op. cit.*, p. 31, pl. vi., figs. 62, 63.

Two living specimens were found at low water on the western side of the Funafuti lagoon.

Fischer† gives as the range of this species New Caledonia, Loyalty Islands, Upolu, Samoa, and Pilsbry adds Fiji.

TROCHUS ATROPURPUREUS, *Gould*.

Pilsbry, *op. cit.*, p. 77, pl. xi., figs. 28–32; pl. xiii., figs. 86, 87; pl. xv., figs. 50, 51.

Not uncommon as dead shells on the lagoon beach.

Pilsbry notes this from San Christoval, Solomons, Tutuila, Samoa and Fiji. In this Museum are specimens from New Caledonia and Tupuselei, Hood Lagoon and Milne Bay, British New Guinea.

TROCHUS FASTIGIATUS, *A. Adams*.

Reeve, Conch. Icon. xiii., 1861, Trochus, pl. xv., fig. 87.

Several dead specimens from the beach of the Funafuti lagoon. Though described nearly half a century ago, the locality of this species has not hitherto been announced. I have also collected it at Panie, New Caledonia.

GIBBULA CONCINNA, *Dunker*.

Pilsbry, *op. cit.*, p. 230, pl. xl., figs. 8, 9.

A shell plentiful at Funafuti and which I also saw at Nukulailai, seems, though not agreeing exactly, to be nearest this. The

---

* Pilsbry—The Nautilus, v., Dec. 1891, p. 88.
† Fischer—Coquilles Vivantes, Trochus, 1880, p. 117.

sculpture and, except for a white apex, the colour, is like that of
G. danieli, Crosse, from which it differs by a crenulate umbilical
margin. The largest is 7½ mm in diameter and has an umbilicus
1½ mm. broad.

G. concinna is known only from Upola, Samoa.

GIBBULA PHASIANELLA, *Deshayes.*

Pilsbry, *op. cit.,* p. 235, pl. xxxi., figs. 31, 32, 33.

Dead shells frequently occurred on the lagoon beach of Funafuti.

Specimens from the Manchester Museum enable me to state that
this is the species which Melvill and Standen record* from Lifu
as "*Margarita striatula,* Phil.," a name which I have been unable
to trace in literature. It has already been recorded from Lifu,
and also from Ile Art by Fischer.† I found it alive in abundance under stones between tide marks, at Noumea, New Caledonia.
It is represented in this Museum from Lord Howe Island.

The species hardly seems suitably placed in this genus.

MONILEA LIFUANA, *Fischer.*

Pilsbry, *op. cit.,* p. 252, pl. xli., figs. 6, 7; pl. lix., figs. 64, 65.

Commonly seen in a dead state on the sandy beach of the
Funafuti lagoon.

As the name implies this species was first found at the Loyalty
Islands. Smith‡ has recorded it from Torres Straits. It is also
in this Museum from Aneiteum, New Hebrides.

MONILEA TRAGEMA, *Melvill & Standen.*

Melvill & Standen, Journ. Conch., viii., 1896, p. 313, pl. xi.,
fig. 78.

A shell fairly plentiful in a dead state on the lagoon beach of
Funafuti is referred here. The fifty examples before me show
much variation. The colour ranges from pale pink articulated
with white, through white irregularly splashed or microscopically
dotted with pink, to entire chalky white. The elevation and
angulation of the whorls vary, and the size of the largest (length
4½ mm.) is almost double that of the type from Lifu.

EUCHELUS INSTRICTUS, *Gould.*

Pilsbry, *op. cit.,* p. 441, pl. lxvii., figs. 62, 63.

A single dead specimen from the beach of the Funafuti
lagoon.

---

* Melvill & Standen—Journ. Conch. viii., 1896, p. 126.
† Fischer, *op. cit.,* p. 364.
‡ Smith—Zool. Coll. "Alert," 1884, p. 73.

Schmeltz quotes this from Fiji and Samoa. There are specimens in this Museum from New Caledonia.

TEINOSTOMA QUALUM, sp. nov.
(Fig. 2).

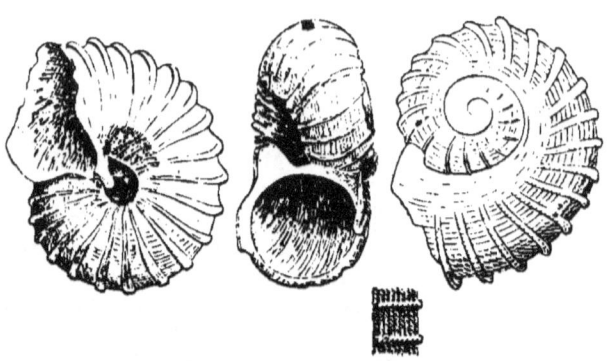

Fig. 2.

Shell with spire scarcely elevated, rather widely umbilicated. Colour white. Whorls three, flattened below the suture, rounded at the periphery and concave at the base. Sculpture :—the last whorl is ornamented by about twenty, broad, squarely projecting, transverse ribs, which arise at a distance from the suture, enlarge to the periphery and continue to the basal angle, these ribs vanish on the penultimate whorl ; close, regular and fine, raised, spiral lines cover the whole shell, crossing the ribs and interstices alike; these are in their turn overridden by transverse microscopic threads. Base excavate in the centre. Umbilicus one-fifth of the shell's diameter, exhibiting the previous whorls. Aperture round, lip thickened, above spreading on the previous whorl and at the base projecting a callus tongue into the umbilicus. Major diameter 1·8; minor 1·4; height ·75.

Three specimens from sand on the lagoon shore, all of which are unfortunately broken at the aperture.

This closely resembles *Cyclostrema archeri*, Tryon* from Singapore, which is rather larger and more closely ribbed, but the basal callus on the lip of the present form has decided me in considering it generically and therefore specifically distinct from that.

TEINOSTOMA TRICARINATA, *Melvill & Standen.*
Melvill & Standen, Journ. Conch., viii., 1896, p. 311, pl. xi., figs. 75 *a. b.*
Three specimens occurred on the sandy beach of the Funafuti lagoon. The only other example known came from Lifu.

---

* Man. Conch. x., 1888, p. 89, pl. xxxiii., figs. 84, 85.

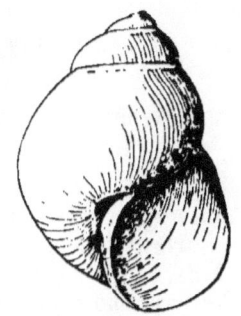

Fig. 3.

CIRSONELLA OVATA, sp. nov.

(Fig. 3).

Shell globose-ovate, thin, and semi-transparent, white, narrowly umbilicate. Whorls five, rounded, smooth, save for delicate growth-striations, margined and contracted below the suture. Aperture oblique, elliptical. Lip sharp, columella reflected. Length, 2½, breadth 2 mm.

Three specimens from the lagoon beach.

LIOTIA CRENATA, *Kiener.*

Tryon, Man. Conch. x., 1888, p. 111, pl. xxxvi., figs. 12, 13.

One shell from the lagoon beach. This is represented in the Australian Museum from Aneitcum, New Hebrides. Smith quotes it from San Christoval, Solomons, and Melvill and Standen from Lifu.

PHASIANELLA WISEMANNI, *Baird.*

Pilsbry, Man. Conch. x., 1888, p. 181, pl. xxxix., figs. 73, 74.

Several specimens from the lagoon beach. Schmeltz unites with this *P. graffei*, Dunker.* Already recorded from the Ellice, Samoa, and Tonga, by Schmeltz. Reported by Pilsbry from Fiji and New Hebrides.

PHASIANELLA MINIMA, *Melvill.*

Melvill, Proc. Malac. Soc. ii., 1896, p. 115, pl. viii., fig. 11.

Three shells from the lagoon beach seem to be referable to this Bombay species.

STOMATELLA SANGUINEA, *A. Adams.*

Pilsbry, Man. Conch. xii., 1890, p. 18, pl. liii., figs. 85, 86.

Common as dead shells on the lagoon beach. Pilsbry notes this species from Fiji, Upolu, Samoa, and the Paumotus; Schmeltz adds Tahiti.

STOMATIA PHYMOTIS, *Helbling.*

Pilsbry, *op. cit.*, p. 31, pl. liv., figs. 16, 17, 21, 22.

Dead shells were not rare on the lagoon beach. Pilsbry records this species from Fiji, and Schmeltz from Upolu. In this Museum it is shown from New Caledonia and the Louisiades.

GENA ROSACEA, *Pease.*

Pilsbry, *op. cit.*, p. 41, pl. lv., fig. 12.

---

* Schmeltz—Museum Godeffroy, Cat. v., 1874, p. 145.

Several empty shells from the lagoon beach. Hitherto only recorded from the Paumotus.

TURBO PETHOLATUS, *L.*, var. CALEDONICUS, *Fischer.*

Pilsbry, Man. Conch. x., 1888, p. 194, pl. xlv., fig. 99.

A few dead shells were collected on the beaches.

This variety, of a peculiar colour pattern, and angled more or less at the shoulder, is recorded by Fischer from New Caledonia, and Anaa, Paumotus. A specimen in this Museum from the Gilbert Islands shares this form and colour. Perhaps the typical form is replaced in the Central Pacific by this variety.

TURBO SETOSUS, *Gmelin.*

Pilsbry, *op. cit.*, p. 195, pl. lxiii., fig. 32.

Abundant on the east coast of the atoll at low water on the outer reef.

Fischer cites this species from New Caledonia, Tahiti, Paumotus, Marquesas, and Gilberts; Schmeltz adds Samoa. It is also shown in this Museum from the Solomons.

The opercula of the Funafuti examples agree with Fischer's description,* but not with Pilsbry's, being white and smooth, except on the distal margin, where they are brown and obliquely wrinkled.

TURBO ARGYROSTOMUS, *Linne.*

Pilsbry, *op. cit.*, p. 197, pl. xl., fig. 18; pl. xlii., fig. 41; pl. xlvi., fig. 8.

This species was less abundant; it replaced the preceding on the western side of the atoll. Fischer indicates it from Tonga, and from Anaa, Paumotus, and Schmeltz from Upolu. It is represented in this Museum from the Solomons, New Caledonia, Fanning Island, and Hawaii.

ASTRALIUM PETROSUM, *Martyn.*

Pilsbry, *op. cit.*, p. 234, pl. lxiv., figs. 65, 66.

I found this alive in the lagoon.

Pilsbry records this from New Caledonia, Fiji, and Hawaii. An example from Woodlark Island, British New Guinea, is in this Museum.

LEPTOTHYRA LAETA, *Montrouzier.*

Pilsbry, *op. cit.*, p. 258, pl. lxiii., figs. 29, 30.

Common on the lagoon beach at Funafuti.

Pilsbry records this from Australia, Solomons, Fiji, and New Caledonia.

---

* Fischer—Coquilles Vivantes, 1873, Turbo, p. 57.

DELPHINULA LACINIATA, *Lamarck.*

Pilsbry, *op. cit.*, p. 266, pl. lxvii., figs. 1, 2, 4.

I collected a single worn shell on the sandbank in the centre of the Funafuti lagoon.

It is recorded by Kiener* from New Ireland, by Melvill and Standen† from the Loyalty, and there is a specimen in this Museum collected by Pére Montrouzier at Woodlark Island, British New Guinea.

NERITOPSIS RADULA, *Linne.*

Tryon, *op. cit.*, p. 82, pl. xxix., fig. 68.

One dead shell was found on the beach.

Melvill and Standen record this from Lifu. Specimens from New Caledonia are described by Fischer.‡

NERITA ALBICILLA, *Linne.*

Martens, Conch. Cab. ii., 11, 1889, p. 25, pl. viii., figs. 1, 2.

One living example, found in the lagoon.

This species ranges south along the Australian coast to Sydney. Von Martens cites Port Carteret, New Ireland, Solomons, New Caledonia, Fiji, Samoa, Tonga, and Tahiti. A specimen from Erromanga, New Hebrides, is in this Museum.

NERITA MAXIMA, *Chemnitz.*

Martens, *op. cit.*, p. 29, pl. vi., figs. 1 – 5.

Two living shells from under stones between tides in the lagoon of Funafuti.

Von Martens quotes for this Jaluit, Marshalls, Fiji, Samoa, and Tahiti.

Specimens are in this Museum from Aneiteum, New Hebrides.

NERITA PLICATA, *Linne.*

Martens, *op. cit.*, p. 63, pl. x., figs. 6 – 10.

This species occured at Funafuti in great profusion. The wave-worn breccia of the outer beach, just above high tide, is its favourite haunt. Here a hundred may be gathered from a few square feet. Into any crevice they crawl and huddle together like a cluster of *Helix aspersa* when hibernating. Their tenacity is wonderful. Often when picking them out of a crevice in the coral, I have pulled away the shell and found the foot and operculum adhering to the rock, torn from the viscera left in the

---

* Kiener—Coquilles Vivantes, 1873. Delphinula, p. 4.
† Melvill & Standen—*Op. cit.*, p. 126.
‡ Fischer—Journ. de Conch. xxiii., 1875, p. 197.

shell. This mollusc sometimes ascends the trunks of trees in the vicinity of the beach, and behaves more like a terrestrial than a marine organism.

Martens quotes the following habitats from the Pacific :—New Guinea, Tucopia, New Caledonia, Fiji, Upolu, Samoa, Uvea, Futuna, Tongatabu, Tahiti, Borabora, Gambier, Paumotus, Marquesas, Jaluit, Marshalls, Ponape, Guam, Carolines, and the Mariannes. Material in this Museum enables me to add Erromanga, New Hebrides, and the Solomons.

At Port Moresby, British New Guinea, I was told that this mollusc is locally called "mimi," meaning "to itch," because it made the tongue of the eater sore.

NERITA POLITA, *Linne.*

Martens, *op. cit.*, p. 72, pl. iii., figs. 5, 10–26; pl. xiv., figs. 1–18, 22–26.

One specimen of the typical form found alive in the lagoon of Funafuti.

Martens cites this from Queensland, New Ireland, Solomons, Fiji, Upolu, Samoa, Vavao, Tonga, Mangarewa, Society Islands, and Hawaii. I can add Eromanga, New Hebrides.

NERITA INSCULPTA, *Recluz.*

Martens, *op. cit.*, p. 88, pl. xi., figs. 1–4.

Two living specimens were found in the Funafuti lagoon.

Martens notices this from Upolu, Samoa, and Bowen, Queensland.

NERITINA RETICULATA, *Sowerby.*

Martens, Conch. Cab. ii., 10, 1879, p. 132, pl. xv., figs. 1–3.

Several dead shells were found on the beach of the Funafuti lagoon.

Martens cites this from Nukuhiva, Marquesas, Tahiti, Bornbora, and Morutea. In this Museum it is reported from Strong Island, New Caledonia, and the Solomons. ·

HELICINA MUSIVA, var. ROTUNDATA, *Mousson.*

Mousson, Journ. de Conch., xxi., 1873, p. 107.

Common at Funafuti. Graeffe collected this at Vaitupu.

EULIMA PYRAMIDALIS, *A. Adams.*

Tryon, Man. Conch., viii., 1886, p. 270, pl. lxviii., fig. 14.

Three examples from the lagoon beach.

I cannot, from published data, separate the later described *E. solida*, Sowb., and *E. inflexa*, Pease. Granted this synonymy, the species extends to Fiji, Paumotus, and Hawaii.

EULIMA DECIPIENS, sp. nov.
(Fig. 4).

Shell small, straight, rather broad, translucent, glossy. Colour porcelainous white. Apex mucronate. Whorls eleven, scarcely rounded, sculpture none. Suture scarcely perceptible ; what first appears to be the suture, proves with further magnification to be the internal septa seen through the shell substance. Aperture pyriform, oblique, with a callous arched columella. Length 5, breadth $1\frac{1}{2}$ mm.

One living specimen from the lagoon.

This species somewhat resembles *E. piriformis*, Brugnone, than which it is rather narrower.

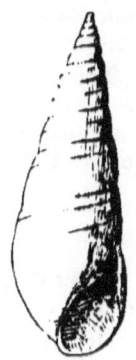

Fig. 4.

STYLIFER VARICIFERUS, sp. nov.
(Fig. 5).

Shell ovate conical, thin, translucent and shining. Apex broken but apparently acicular. Remaining whorls nine, of which the

Fig. 5.

latter are markedly tumid and narrow, giving the shell a squeezed or telescoped aspect. The upper whorls are smooth and polished, the lower gradually acquire an oblique, longitudinal sculpture which becomes coarser as the shell proceeds and finally on the last half whorl rise into sharp varices; on the latter three whorls several weak spiral threads reticulate the transverse growth lines and create angles below the suture and the periphery. Aperture very oblique, lip sharp, sinuous, reflected, effuse anteriorly, columella broad, arched, and reflected over a minute perforation. Length 11, breadth 6½ mm.

This species in size and general shape approaches *S. eburneus*, Deshayes. But in the produced and effuse aperture it recedes from that towards *S. crotaphis*, Watson. A single specimen was procured at Funafuti.

ODOSTOMIA BULIMOIDES, *Souverbie.*

Tryon, *op. cit.*, p. 362, pl. lxxix., fig. 69.

Several specimens which appear to be the young of this species from the lagoon beach.

Described by Souverbie from New Caledonia and reported by Melvill and Standen from Lifu.

ODOSTOMIA RUBRA, *Pease.*

Tryon, *op. cit.*, p. 363, pl. lxxix., fig. 75.

One living example from the lagoon. Pease procured the type from the Paumotus.

PYRAMIDELLA DOLABRATA, var. TEREBELLOIDES, *A. Adams.*

Tryon, *op. cit.*, p. 300, pl. lxxii., fig. 74.

Two dead shells from the lagoon. There are specimens of this in the Museum from Hawaii, under the name of *Obeliscus sulcatus*, Nuttall.

PYRAMIDELLA TURRITA, *A. Adams.*

Tryon, *op. cit.*, p. 301, pl. lxxii., figs. 84, 85.

A few dead shell from the lagoon beach. Tryon records this from New Caledonia.

In these two latter species, aged or adult individuals develop plicæ within the lip, a fact omitted in monographs.

PYRAMIDELLA MITRALIS, *A. Adams.*

Tryon, *op. cit.*, p. 305, pl. lxxiii., figs. 2, 3, 94, 97.

Two dead shells from the lagoon beach. Tryon quotes this from Tahiti; Melvill and Standen from Lifu. In this Museum it it represented from Guam, New Caledonia, and Lord Howe Island.

OBTORTIO, gen. nov.

A shell of the Turbonillidæ, small, conical. Apex of two minute discoidal whorls, half buried in a larger and longitudinally ribbed whorl, to which succeeds a ribbed and tabulate whorl; these together constituting a mu on te tip. On the next whorl, which is also tabulate, he longitudinal sculpture almost disappears and spiral lyræ arise. Subsequently these latter are cancelled by a reappearance of the longitudinal ribs. Aperture oval with a broad and reflected columella, no varix.

Type *Rissoa pyrrhacme*, Melvill & Standen.

ORTORTIO PYRRHACME, *Melvill & Standen.*
Fig. 6.

Melvill & Standen, Journ. Conch., viii., 1896, p. 310, pl. xi., fig. 70.

These authors describe from Lifu, Loyalty Islands : " A pure white ochre tipped shell, whorls eight or nine, much swollen, longitudinally ribbed, spirally closely sulcate, aperture round, lip simple, a little effuse." This account is illustrated by a figure too small to give details of sculpture, aperture or apex. To identify a species from such data is a little hazardous, but the brown point to the white shell is a peculiar feature which leads me to see in "*Rissoa pyrrhacme*" a common New Caledonian shell, long known to the local collectors under the, doubtless erroneous, name of "*Fenella pupoides*, Adams."* I have collected this at Panie, New Caledonia, a day's sail from Lifu, whence Melvill and Standen derived *Rissoa pyrrhacme.*

Among shell sand on the lagoon beach of Funafuti I gathered a dozen specimens specifically inseparable from the Panie shells which I thus identified. They are smaller than Melvill and Standen's specimens, being barely four millimetres in length, whereas theirs are six, the tips, unlike my Panie examples, are faintly and barely touched with colour, as if singed by fire. In contour they exhibit much variety ; two examples are drawn

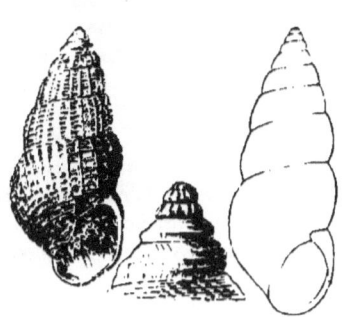

Fig. 6.

to the same scale to illustrate diversity of proportion, perhaps a sexual feature. The apex, which I hold to exhibit characters of generic importance, consists first of two very minute whorls which are almost buried in the succeeding whorl. These are very difficult to observe, being seen in two instances only in the series examined. A globose whorl, longitudinally ribbed, sometimes only obliquely wrinkled, commences the real spire. This, the subsequent whorl and the tip, together form an acicular point to the shell when viewed through a hand-lens. The second, third, and fourth whorls are tabulate, lending a pagoda aspect to the

---

* *Cf.* Schmeltz—Cat. Godeffroy Museum, v., 1874, p. 104.

upper spire. These are the whorls stained chestnut, so dark as to be almost black, in the New Caledonian specimens. The larger whorls are closely corded by spiral lyræ, having smaller lyræ in their interstices. Weak, longitudinal ribs undulate the central whorls and appear on the last whorl, but vanish there before reaching the periphery. The columella lip is broad and reflected, obliquely ridged within and sharply bent above. The aperture is perpendicular, ovate and grooved within.

Rissoa joviana of Melvill and Standen* appears to me to be an absolute synonym of *Alaba fulva*, Watson.† These and *Alaba striata*, Watson‡ should enter the same genus as *pyrrhacme*. Indeed I am not satisfied that all four names do not apply to aspects of one polymorphic species.

SCALA REVOLUTA, sp. nov.
(Fig. 7).

Fig. 7.

Shell minute, white, with smooth coiled apex and variced, solute, subsequent whorls. Whorls six, of which the apical three are smooth and in contact, the fourth commences to uncoil and the remainder are widely separate. Varices eight on the last whorl, with an anterior corner, slightly elevated ; between the varices the shell is smooth and glossy. Aperture broken in the type example, but apparently circular. Length 3, breadth 1·5 mm.

One specimen from the lagoon beach.

The only shell for which the novelty might be mistaken is *S. hyalina*, Sowerby. Judging from Sowerby's drawings§ that differs by being much larger, broader, uncoiled to the tip, though less apart latterly, and by more numerous and serrate varices.

SCALA PAUMOTENSIS, *Pease.*

Tryon, Man. Conch. ix., 1887, p. 65, pl. xiii., fig. 16.

Four specimens from the lagoon beach. Cited by Tryon from Fiji, Gilberts, and Paumotus.

SCALA SUBAURICULATA, *Souverbie.*

Tryon, *op. cit.*, p. 67, pl. xiv., figs. 21, 22.

Four specimens from the lagoon beach correspond fairly well with New Caledonian examples.

---

* *Op. cit.*, p. 309, pl. xi., fig. 69.
† Chall. Report, xv., 1886, p. 571, pl. xlii., figs. 5 a. b.
‡ *Op. cit.*, 569, pl. xlii., figs. 6 a. b.
§ Thesaurus Conch. I., 1847, pl. xxxii., figs. 21, 22.

SCALA OVALIS, *Sowerby*.

Tryon, *op. cit.*, p. 69, pl. xiv., fig. 40.

With doubt I refer here a species obtained on the lagoon shore.

SCALIOLA LAPILLIFERA, sp. nov.
(Fig. 8).

Shell ovate conical, broad for the genus, white, thin and translucent. Whorls seven, rounded, the earlier closely coiled, the later looser, surface obscurely marked by growth striæ. Apical whorls smooth and bare ; the rest beset with adherent sand grains more closely disposed about and below the periphery. Aperture round, free from the preceding whorl, with expanded and reflected lip. Length 2, breadth 1 mm.

Fig. 8.

Three examples from the sandy beach of the lagoon.

This is smaller and proportionately broader than other *Scaliola* and especially differs by the almost solute whorls. It is less coated with adherent matter than *S. caledonica*.

IANTHINA, sp.

Specimens of an *Ianthina* too young to determine specifically occurred on the outer beach.

NATICA VIOLACEA, *Sowerby*.

Tryon, Man. Conch. viii., 1886, p. 18, pl. iii., fig. 41.

One dead and broken example from the beach of the lagoon.

Tryon quotes this from Fiji ; Melvill and Standen from Lifu. In this Museum it is represented from the Bampton Reef, Coral Sea and New Caledonia.

NATICA MAROCHIENSIS, *Gmelin*.

Tryon, *op. cit.*, p. 22, pl. v., figs. 74–96 ; pl. vii., fig. 36 ; pl. viii., fig. 49.

Several dead shells occurred on the lagoon beach.

Melvill and Standen quote this from Lifu. In this Museum its Australian range is shown to be from Torres Straits to Sydney, and it is also represented from the New Hebrides, New Caledonia and Hawaii.

NATICA MAMILLA, *Linne*.

Tryon, *op. cit.*, p. 49, pl. xv., fig. 43 ; pl. xvi., figs. 46, 48 ; pl xvii., figs. 65, 69.

One specimen was obtained attached to a native ornament as described ante p. 247.

This Museum contains representatives from Queensland, British New Guinea, New Caledonia and Hawaii.

NATICA MELANOSTOMA, *Gmelin.*

Tryon, *op. cit.*, p. 50, pl. xxi., figs. 13–18; pl. xxii., fig. 21.

A few empty shells were picked up on the beach of the lagoon.

Examples from Eagle Island, Queensland, British New Guinea and New Caledonia are shown in this Museum.

NATICA UMBILICATA, *Quoy & Gaimard.*

Tryon, *op. cit.*, p. 52, pl. xxii., fig. 26.

Several dead shells, not specifically distinguishable from this Australian species, were collected on the beach of the lagoon.

The Museum series show it to range from Adelaide to Sydney.

VANIKORO GUERINIANA, *Recluz.*

Tryon, *op. cit.*, p. 68, pl. xxix., fig. 62.

Several specimens were found alive in a crevice on the outer reef at low tide.

CAPULUS INTORTUS, *Lamarck.*

Tryon, Man. Conch. viii., 1886, p. 131, pl. xxxix., figs. 75, 76.

Several dead shells were collected on the beach of the lagoon.

Tyron quotes this from the Paumotus, and Melvill and Standen from Lifu. It is preserved in this Museum from Norfolk Island and Aneiteum, New Hebrides.

CAPULUS VIOLACEUS, *Angas.*

Tryon, *op. cit.*, p. 132, pl. xxxix., fig. 81.

Several specimens were gathered dead on the lagoon beach.

Examples of this species are before me from Sydney Harbour and the New Hebrides.

HIPPONYX AUSTRALIS, *Quoy.*

Tryon, *op. cit.*, p. 136, pl. xli., figs. 9–15.

Only found alive as a commensal on the opercula of the large *Pteroceras*.

Tryon cites this from Fiji and New Guinea, and Melvill and Standen from Lifu. It is in this Museum from Torres Straits.

MITRULARIA EQUESTRIS, var. TORTILIS, *Reeve.*

Tryon, *op. cit.*, p. 138, pl. xliii., figs. 53–59, 61–67.

Common dead in the high tide driftage on the shore of the lagoon. Once found alive in a crevice of a coral block.

TRUNCATELLA VALIDA, *Pfeiffer*.

Pfeiffer, Zeits. Malak.,1846, p. 182; Conch. Cab., i., "Truncatella,"
1855, p. 11, pl. ii., figs. 7, 8, 19, 20, 21, 23.
Truncatella vitiana, Gould, Moll., U.S. Explor. Exped., 1852, p.
109, pl. viii., figs. 126, 126a, 126b.

Abundant at Funafuti where it has already been found by
Graeffe.* This belongs to a semi-marine, semi-terrestrial assemblage of which I have already written that—"The smallest islands
which possess any life at all are usually stocked by these forms,
which appear to range from Ceylon in the west, to the Sandwich
Islands in the east, and to be limited north and south by the
tropics."†

Gould remarked that *T. vitiana*, admitted to be variable in
size, "is not very different from *T. valida*." The differences in
sculpture, small perforation, basal keel and posterior fusion of the
ribs, on which he relied to separate the two, are shown by a series
before me to be quite inconstant features. Smith says,‡ "When
the genus is re-monographed, it is probable that some older name
will be discovered to replace that of *valida*." A sentence which
admirably expresses the assistance tendered by London writers
to students of the Pacific Mollusca.

OMPHALOTROPIS ZEBRIOLATA, *Mousson*.

Mousson, Journ. de Conch., xiii., 1865, p. 181, pl. xiv., fig. 11; xxi.,
1873, p. 108 ; Garrett, Proc. Zool. Soc., 1887, p. 308.
Omphalotropis rotumana, Smith, Ann. Mag. Nat. Hist., (6). xx.,
1897, p. 552.

Abundant under sticks and stones on the main islet of Funafuti.
It had already been found here by Graeffe, who also observed it
at Nukufetau, Vaitupu, and Niutao in the Ellice, Nukuiona,
Uvea, Kanathia, Fiji, and Wallis Island. Authentic specimens
of the unfigured *O. rotomana* enable me to confidently unite
this with Mousson's species. Some such conclusion seems indeed
to have been anticipated by Smith, who alludes to this and others
as likely to "eventually prove to be slight variations of already
known species."

ASSIMINEA NITIDA, *Pease*.

Garrett, Proc. Zool. Soc., 1887, p. 314.

Abundant on Funafuti, where it had already been collected by
Graeffe.

Garrett, who gives a complete bibliography says : "This small
species is generally distributed throughout all the groups from the
Paumotus to the Viti Islands and New Caledonia."

---

* Mousson—Journ. de Conch. xxi., 1873, p. 109.
† Hedley—Proc. Linn. Soc. N.S.W. (2) vi., 1891, p. 101.
‡ Smith—Journ. Malak. v., 1896, p. 21.

Cc

RISSOA INVISIBILIS, sp. nov.
(Fig. 9).

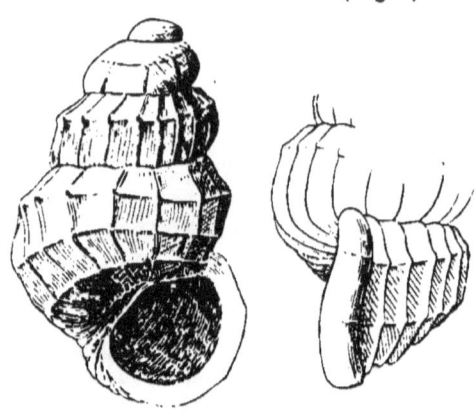

Shell small, sturdy, conic ovate. Colour white. Whorls four. Sculpture — distant, longitudinal, sharp costæ are crossed by three similar spiral ribs, which together divide the surface into nearly square compartments ; at the intersections are small projections. One spiral ridge alone appears on the penultimate whorl,

Fig. 9.

both it and the longitudinals vanish on the whorl above. The base is flattened, umbilicus narrow and deep. Aperture round, columella slightly sinuate, recurved over the umbilicus, lip with a heavy varix. Length 1·15, breadth ·63 mm.

One specimen from the sand of the lagoon shore.

Shape and sculpture ally this to the group including *R. trajectus*, Watson. The heavy lip, open pattern of ornament, and comparative breadth of the shell clearly distinguish the novelty, one of the smallest of the genus, from any known form.

RISSOINA EXASPERATA, *Souverbie*.
(Fig. 10).

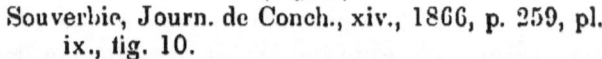

Souverbie, Journ. de Conch., xiv., 1866, p. 259, pl. ix., fig. 10.

To this species is referred with doubt a series from Funafuti. The published account is insufficient for accurate determination, and my principal reason for considering the Ellice shell to be *R. exasperata* is its identity with a common New Caledonian shell which I have myself collected at Panie, N.C., and have received from Noumea, from Mr. R. C.

Fig. 10.

Rossiter. That Conchologist regards it as *R. exasperata*, and it answers fairly to Souverbie's description as far as that goes, but it is less easy to reconcile it with his figure.

This figure, perhaps drawn from a worn specimen, was so badly copied by Weinkauff* as to almost eliminate the name character and represents a smooth *exasperata*. Tryon unfortunately appears

---

* Conchylien Cabinet, i., 22, 1885, p. 54, pl. xiv., fig. 10.

to have accepted the copy, bad beyond recognition, as original, and copied it* in preference to Souverbie's. To the habitat he adds Fiji.

As a synonym I would add the name of *Rissoina quasillus*, Melvill and Standen† from Lifu. Neither figure nor description of this are sufficient for decision, we are not told how many ribs there are, whether continuous or discontinuous, etc., yet there seems nothing incompatible between *R. quasillus* and the shell under discussion. That these authors should have failed to institute a comparison between their supposed novelty and a shell so similar from the same locality, suggests that they overlooked Souverbie's description.

Since so much confusion has enveloped *R. exasperata*, it is not superfluous to present a drawing (Fig. 10) and remarks upon the Funafuti specimens.

Shell elongated, when well preserved slightly turriculated, varies slightly in being more slender or more stout. Dead shells are white. A fresh specimen has within the aperture four narrow, spiral lines of golden brown ; outside, another such line colours the anterior spiral lyra of the antipenultimate whorl, two such the second and third of the penultimate, and three such the second, third, and fifth lyræ respectively of the ultimate whorl. Other worn specimens show traces of this colour pattern. On the last whorl there are nineteen or twenty stout, narrow, erect, longitudinal ribs, half the breadth of their interstices ; these arise at the suture, and maintain an even size to the base, on attaining which they suddenly cease. These ribs are repeated on the preceding whorls ; they are not continuous from whorl to whorl, but each arises and ends between the projections of predecessors and successors. They are fewer and relatively stronger on the earlier whorls, being indicated on the second and fully developed on the fourth.

On the last whorl there are five spiral cords, which are half the height of the longitudinal ribs. At the point of intersection a bead arises on the ribs. The hollows in the lattice work thus formed are square and are minutely spirally striated. The base is encircled by two or three small and finely beaded lyræ. Three spiral cords ascend for three whorls, growing weaker as they proceed. The first whorl is dome-shaped, and the second keeled.

These specimens are $2\frac{1}{2}$ to $3\frac{1}{2}$ mm. long, and have seven to eight whorls.

Occurred in the lagoon in shallow water.

The Chevert Expedition reported this species from Palm and Darnley Islands, Queensland. The Museum also possesses a series presented by Mrs. J. G. Waterhouse, who collected them at Lord Howe

---

* Tryon—Man. Conch., ix., 1887, p. 384, pl. lvii., fig. 96.
† Melvill & Standen—Journ. Conch., viii., 1897, p. 308, pl. xi., fig. 65.

Island. These measure 5 mm. in length, and have an additional spiral cord.

Though certainly distinct, *R. transenna*, Watson, has much resemblance to this species. *R. clathrata*, Adams, appears to differ slightly by coarser sculpture.

RISSOINA GEMMEA, sp. nov.
(Fig. 11).

Shell narrow, conical, white. Whorls eight (including two embryonic), rounded, suture lightly impressed. Embryonic whorls smooth, shining, apparently two, but a study of several species of the genus suggests that the topmost apparent whorl may contain several whorls wound in the same plane and concealed within the outermost. Sculpture—the last whorl is evenly and closely latticed by the intersection of eleven slender spiral cords, and about forty-two delicate longitudinal ribs; a smooth shining bead marks each crossing of the sculpture. The longitudinal ribs are slightly stronger than the spiral cords, a quarter of the breadth of their interstices, slightly oblique and curved; they cross regularly from base to suture and continue without stoppage at the suture, from whorl to whorl of the spire. Ascending the upper whorls, the spiral cords become fewer and gradually vanish leaving as vestiges a few denticles on the ribs. The spaces enclosed by the major sculpture are square shallow pits, spirally striated. Round the base are wound three or four irregularly beaded cords.

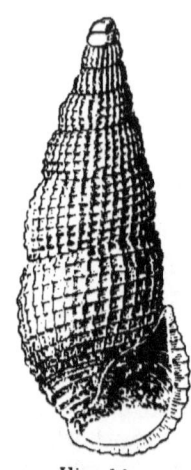

Fig. 11.

Aperture oblique, produced in front, contracted anteriorly to a short spout; columella sharply recurved at the base, extending across the body-whorl as a thick layer of callus; posteriorly the lip is sharply folded at its junction with the body whorl. The outer lip is much thickened, grooved upon the inner face, denticulate on the profile and with a heavy callus behind. Length 4, breadth $1\frac{1}{2}$ mm.

One specimen in shallow water in the lagoon.

In this species the grains seem to be smaller and more numerous than in any other beaded *Rissoina* described.

RISSOINA POLYTROPA, sp. nov.
(Fig. 12).

Shell ovate, fusiform, narrow, white. Suture impressed. Whorls seven, including two embryonic. The last whorl descends from the spiral plane of its predecessors until reaching the aperture, when it ascends suddenly and rapidly, the varix mounting up the preceding whorl for three tiers of spiral lyræ. The shell is thus thrown out of symmetry with most *Rissoina*. Sculpture—as usual with the genus, the longitudinal sculpture predominates to begin with ; the third, or first sculptured, whorl showing a few stout plications. On the following whorl fine spiral threads are visible in the interstices ; on the whorl beneath these are magnified to substantial lyræ ; and on the next or penultimate they have doubled in number, and rival the longitudinal in stature, at their intersection beads appear. On the last whorl the longitudinal, as such, have faded away, their influence showing in fine beads perceptible on the sutural and less distinct on a few of the nearer lyræ; the spiral lyræ have now increased to nearly thirty, the anterior smooth, the posterior with evanescent beading. These are sharply raised threads, half the width of their interstices, evenly arranged, extending from the suture to the anterior point of the shell where they are smaller and more crowded. Aperture almost perpendicular, oval, anteriorly with a short perpendicular spout which falls short of the anterior margin ; columella broad, obliquely and sharply truncated. From this truncation a wide and thick callus extends across the body whorl to the posterior angle of the aperture. Here the lip is sharply bent. The outer bevelled lip projects broadly as a heavy varix crossed by fifteen of the spiral lyræ, the central couple of which are smaller and nearer together. Length $4\frac{1}{2}$, breadth 2 mm.

Fig. 12.

Five specimens in shallow water in the lagoon.

The extinction of longitudinal and the supremacy of spiral sculpture is unfrequent in the genus. Such species have been separated by Nevill as the Section *Morchiella*. From all there included the novelty differs by smaller size, more numerous lyræ, and truncated columella.

RISSOINA PLICATA, *Adams*.
(Fig. 13).

Adams, Proc. Zool. Soc., 1851, p. 264 ; Mohrenstern, Denk. Akad. Wiss., xix., 1860, p. 125, pl. iii., fig. 21 ; Weinkauff, Conch. Cab., i., 22, 1885, p. 23, pl. viii., figs. 5, 6.

Rissoina turricula, Pease, Proc. Zool. Soc., 1860, p. 438.

Two specimens from Funafuti are thus determined. The species appears to vary greatly in size. Whereas the type is described as being $5\frac{1}{2}$ mm. long, the Ellice examples are but $2\frac{1}{2}$ mm. The

Fig. 13.

development of the basal rib, and the number of longitudinal plications vary also. The transverse markings are not grooves, as Adams' description would mislead one to suppose, but elevated threads. The difficulty I found in naming this species induces me to offer a drawing for the assistance of others.

Authentic specimens of *R. turricula*, Pease, from Hawaii, enable me to unite it with the above, a conclusion which Weinkauff's bad figures would not have suggested.

A specimen from British New Guinea is contained in this Museum. Tryon quotes *R. turricula* from Fiji.

RISSOINA AMBIGUA, *Gould*.

Gould, Moll., U.S. Explor. Exped., p. 217, pl. xv., figs. 261*a* – *c*; Tryon, Man. Conch., ix., 1887, p. 371, pl. lv., figs. 27, 29, 31, 35; pl. liv., fig. 7.

A few worn specimens were collected on the lagoon beach. They belong to a variety with smaller and more numerous ribs on the last whorl than the type.

This is one of the most abundant and widespread species in the Pacific. It was first found in the Paumotus Group. I have seen specimens from Tahiti. Pease found it in the Hawaiian and Garrett in the Fijian Islands. I have collected it in Port Moresby, New Guinea, and again at Panie, New Caledonia.

RISSOINA AFFINIS, *Garrett*.

Garrett, Proc. Acad. Nat. Sci. Phil., 1873, p. 212, pl. ii., fig. 10.

One specimen from the lagoon beach resembles Garrett's figure and description, but differs in being microscopically striated above and below the periphery, and also in being eight instead of 5 mm. long.

RISSOINA SPIRATA, var. SUPRACOSTATA, *Garrett*.

Garrett, *loc. cit.*, p. 209, pl. ii., fig. 1; Tryon, *loc. cit.*, p. 388.

A small specimen, even more drawn out than Garrett's figure, from the lagoon beach.

DIALA VIRGATA, sp. nov.
(Fig. 14).

Shell imperforate, narrow, regularly conical, obtusely angled at the periphery, blunt at the tip, surface dull. Colour most variable, typically about half-a-dozen broad, irregular, opaque, white stripes extend longitudinally upon a translucent white ground from the suture to beyond the periphery of the last whorl, and cross the full breadth of the earlier ones. The translucent ground, but not the opaque patches, are crossed by an indefinite number, commonly

from eight to sixteen, spiral brown threads.
These lines sometimes coalesce and produce a
colour pattern of opaque white blotches on
a dark chestnut ground. The opaque white
spaces vary in number and extent; when restricted they appear as a series of rhombs
on the periphery and triangles on the suture;
by confluence these form longitudinal ragged
stripes and separate the barred or brown
tracts into rough ovals. This colouration is
visible within the aperture. Sculpture—
longitudinal growth lines are perceptible;
the whole body whorl is evenly spaced by

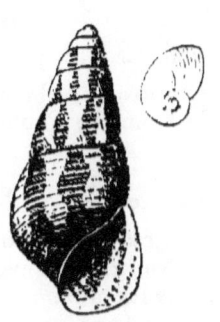

Fig. 14.

about a dozen, wide, very shallow grooves, upon the narrow in-
tervening ridges of which are apt to occur the chestnut bars; the
peripheral groove is the most distinct. Whorls seven, gradually
increasing, slightly rounded; embryonic whorl one, minute, turbinate. Suture deeply impressed. Aperture slightly oblique,
ovate, pointed posteriorly, rounded and effuse anteriorly; columella reflected, stained medially with chestnut; callus on body
whorl slight, outer lip straight, simple. Operculum thin, corneous,
ovate, paucispiral. Length 2¾, breadth 1¼ mm.

Very abundant; alive on stones and shells in shallow water in
the lagoon.

This species differs from *D. albugo*, Watson, and *D. ludens*,
Melvill and Standen, by a dull instead of a glossy surface, and
by the opaque tracts occurring in larger continuous sheets instead
of being scattered in small and numerous dots.

From the description of *Rissoa flammea*, Pease,* I suppose that
it is either the same or very like the shell before me.

DIALA HARDYI, *Melvill & Standen.*

Melvill & Standen, Journ. Conch., viii., 1895, p. 118, pl. ii.,
fig. 10.

This species is common in the lagoon. I have identified it with
a species I took at Panie, New Caledonia, which answers to the
account of the Lifu shell.

SOLARIUM HYBRIDUM, *Linne.*

Tryon, Man. Conch. ix., 1887, p. 14, pl. v., figs. 59 – 62.

A dead example from the lagoon beach.

Recognised by Melvill and Standen from Lifu, by Schmeltz
from Samoa, Tonga, and Cook's Islands, and represented in this
Museum from Teste Island, Louisiades.

---

* Pease—Am. Journ. Conch., iii., 1867, p. 207, pl. xxiv., fig. 33.

HELIACUS DISCOIDEUS, *Pease*.

Tryon, *loc. cit.*, p. 21, pl. vi., fig. 6.

One dead shell from the shore of the lagoon. Previously known only from the Paumotus.

LITTORINA OBESA, *Sowerby*.

Tryon, *loc. cit.*, p. 247, pl. xliii., fig. 53.

In great profusion at and above high water-mark, on stones and even tree stems, on the windward beach of the atoll, in company with *Nerita*, *Truncatella*, and *Melampus*.

Recorded by Melvill and Standen from Lifu, by Smith* from Rotuma, and shown in this Museum from Eddystone Island (Solomons), Vate (New Hebrides), the Gilberts, and Fanning Island.

MODULUS TECTUM, *Gmelin.*

Tryon, *loc. cit*, p. 260, pl. xlviii., figs. 87–89.

One dead shell was found on the beach of the Funafuti lagoon.

Tryon quotes this from Fiji and Hawaii; Melvill and Standen from Lifu. It is in this Museum from New Caledonia.

RISELLA CONOIDALIS, *Pease*.

Tryon, *loc. cit.*, p. 263, pl. l., fig. 38.

Dead shells were not uncommon on the sandy beach of the lagoon.

The species was originally described from the Paumotus. I have collected it at Panie, New Caledonia. Schmeltz mentions it from Tahiti. There can, I think, be little doubt that the shell described twelve years later from Lifu by Montrouzier† as *Echinella gaidei* is identical.

PLESIOTROCHUS SOUVERBIANUS, *Fischer*.

Tryon, *loc. cit.*, p. 264, pl. l., figs. 44–46.

Not rare as dead shells on the sandy shore of the lagoon. Originally described from Lifu.

FOSSARUS LAMELLOSUS, *Montrouzier*.

Tryon, *loc. cit.*, p. 271, pl. lii., fig. 7.

Three dead shells were found on the beach of the Funafuti lagoon. The type from New Caledonia is described as imperforate, but these have a deep and narrow umbilicus.

PLANAXIS SULCATUS, *Born*.

Tryon, *lo.c cit.*, p. 276, pl. lii., figs. 22–27, 31, 32.

---

* Smith—Ann. Mag. Nat. Hist., (6) xx., 1897, p. 523.
† Montrouzier—Journ. de Conch., xxvii., 1879, p. 62, pl. iii., figs. 3, 3a.

I found this gregarious species in great numbers under stones between tide marks on the lagoon shore of Funafuti. Tenison Woods has described this as occurring in similar positions and abundance in tropical Queensland.*

In this Museum it is represented from Torres Straits and Port Molle, Queensland, and the Solomons.

PLANAXIS LINEATUS, *Da Costa.*

Tryon, *loc. cit.*, p. 278, pl. liii., figs. 49 – 57, 59, 63 – 66; pl. lii., figs. 38 – 48.

This species is also markedly gregarious. Little colonies occurred under stones between tide marks on the outer reef of Funafuti.

Tryon mentions this from the Solomons, Tahiti and Paumotus. Melvill and Standen record it under the synonym of *P. virgatus*, Smith, from Lifu. Smith gives it from Fiji.† I have collected it at Oubatche, New Caledonia, and this Museum has it from Hawaii and the New Hebrides.

MELANIA MAGENI, *Gassies.*

Gassies, Faune Conchyliologique de la Nouvelle Caledonie, 1863, part i., p. 95, pl. vi., fig. 10.

Abundant in the native wells at Funafuti.

First described from New Caledonia, and lately recognised by Smith from Rotuma. Contrary to the priority given by Brot and Crosse this species has page precedence over *M. montrouzieri*, Gassies.

CAECUM VERTEBRALE, sp. nov.

(Fig. 15).

Caecum sp., De Folin, Challenger Reports, Zoology, xv., 1886, p. 684, pl. ii., fig. 12.

Shell of moderate size for the genus, white (? bleached), rather curved, slightly tapering, ornamented with twenty-five strong, pretty regular rounded, transverse rings, which are separated by interstices of corresponding breadth and depth. Septum a low rounded dome. Length 2·15, breadth ·56 mm.

A single perfect specimen, gathered on the sandy shore of the lagoon, is with some confidence identified with a nameless fragment dredged by the "Challenger" off Honolulu.

Fig. 15.

* Tenison Woods—Proc. Linn. Soc. N. S.W., v., 1881, p. 108.
† Smith—Journ. Linn. Soc., Zool., xii., 1876, p. 552.

CAECUM EXILE, *De Folin.*

De Folin, *loc. cit.*, p. 687, pl. iii., figs. 20 – 22.

Four specimens of this were collected with the preceding. That two are a pale umber colour suggests that the unique shell dredged by the "Challenger" off Tongatabu and described as crystalline, was faded. I have also taken this at Panie, New Caledonia.

CAECUM GULOSUM, sp. nov.

(Fig. 16).

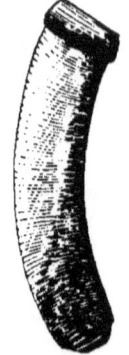

Shell white, slender, rather curved, suddenly expanded behind the aperture, concentrically sculptured by fine close threads which grow coarser anteriorly. Septum much exserted, flattened distally and with two rough ring ridges. Length 1·8, breadth ·4 mm.

One specimen from the lagoon beach.

Nearest to *C. attenuatum* which is narrower and more curved, also allied to *C. amputatum*, Hedley,[*] from which it differs by being smaller and of a more slender build.

Fig. 16.

VERMETUS MAXIMUS, *Sowerby.*

(Fig. 17).

Tryon, Man. Conch. viii., 1886, p. 184, pl. lv., figs. 89, 90 ; Morch, Proc. Zool. Soc. 1861, p. 166.

The Funafuti people consider this species good food, and call it "gea." It occurs in abundance in large clumps of Millepora growing on the lagoon side of the southern horn of the main islet. Here the earlier and irregularly coiled whorls were imbedded in the coral mass, but the last half foot of the tube stood up erect and free. What I consider the same species also grew, though rarely, on the outer reef-flat at low water, where it was altogether prostrate and had a more pronounced keel.

One fine specimen is thirty-five mm. across the aperture. Within the shell is white, smooth and porcellanous, at the slightly everted lip it has a faint purple tinge which soon fades. Externally it has a longitudinal, dorsal keel or crest, and is concentrically furrowed by growth lines. The distal part of the tube is, perhaps as a repair after injury, sometimes plugged with a shelly wad.

The animal is bold and active, if touched it shrinks two or three inches down the tube, but soon recovers confidence and rises to the aperture. The mantle margin is sometimes entire, sometimes notched dorsally. The long thick retractor or columella muscle is ventral.

---

[*] Hedley—Proc. Linn. Soc. N.S.W., (2) viii., 1893, p. 504, fig.

Beneath the head is a flap terminating anteriorly in two processes and arising from a deep cleft between the mouth and the operculum. Treating of the same or an allied species from Guam, Quoy and Gaimard* describe this as an anti-buccal appendage and figure it from above. I regard it as the relic of a degenerated propodium. The accompanying sketch (Fig. 17) in profile, of an animal half drawn out of the shell and stript of the operculum, will better convey an idea of this organ than figures taken from above.

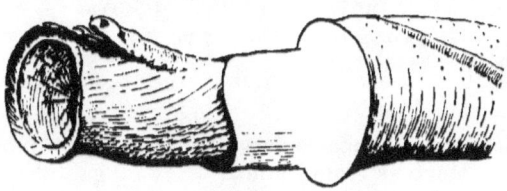

Fig. 17.

When a gasteropod retreats into the shell it doubles the foot either lengthwise, as in some inoperculate forms, or across, as in most operculates. In the latter case when completely retracted, the foot is so folded head to tail that the anterior half of the sole is applied to the posterior; the operculum then closes the aperture. In a sedentary form this position of retraction might become permanent. Where the foot never serves for progression, but continues to maintain a useful operculum, it is easy to imagine that the fore part of the folded foot would become atrophied and that as it diminished the hind part would enlarge. This is the history suggested for the shrunken propodium of *Vermetus*, which lies tucked away between the mouth and the operculum. The process of evolution perhaps continued in the direction of utilising the appendices of the propodium as tentacles.

This species was collected by Hugh Cuming at Marutea, Paumotus, and opercula of it were received from Lifu by Melvill and Standen. In a preceding article (p. 243) I have quoted a description of a mollusc from Mangaiia, called "ungakoa," which is probably this. In Java it is known as "karang," which Morch translates as "coral tube." The only Pacific shell with which this can be confused is the pipe-like *Kuphus arenarius,* L.

VERMETUS, sp.

A second species of this genus, somewhat resembling *V. grandis,* Gray,† or *V. imbricatus,* Dunker, also occurred.

TURRITELLA CONCAVA, *Martens.*
Tryon, *loc. cit.,* p. 206, pl. lxiv., fig. 6.

---

* Quoy & Gaimard—Voy. "Astrolabe," Zoologie, iii., 1835, p. 295, pl. lxvii., figs. 13 - 15.
† Tryon—Man. Conch., viii., 1886, p. 182, pl. liv., fig. 79.

Two imperfect shells from the lagoon correspond to examples of this Mauritian species.

STROMBUS LENTIGINOSUS, *Linne.*

Tryon, Man. Conch. vii., 1885, p. 110, pl. iii., figs. 23, 24.

One dead shell I picked up on the Funafuti beach.

Tryon gives the localities of New Caledonia and Fiji; in this Museum it is from British New Guinea and the Solomons.

STROMBUS FLORIDUS, *Lamarck.*

Tryon, *loc. cit.*, p. 119, pl. vii., figs. 73 - 76, 80, 83.

Abundant alive in shallow water in the lagoon, associated with *S. luhuanus.*

Cuming saw this in the Society Islands, Tryon quotes it from Fiji, and Von Martens from Samoa.* It ranges along the Australian coast south to Sydney. In this Museum it is represented from Teste Island, Louisiades, Erromanga, New Hebrides, and Hawaii.

STROMBUS DENTATUS, var. RUGOSUS, *Sowerby.*

Tryon, *loc. cit.*, p. 119, pl. vii., fig. 72.

Abundant alive in the Funafuti lagoon.

Schmeltz records this from Samoa and Tonga.†

STROMBUS HÆMASTOMA, *Sowerby.*

Tryon, *loc. cit.*, p. 120, pl. vii., fig. 78.

Recorded from the Ellice Group by Schmeltz.‡

STROMBUS TEREBELLATUS, *Sowerby.*

Tryon, *loc. cit.*, p. 121, pl. viii., fig. 87.

Alive, with the preceding, but uncommon.

Tryon notes this from Fiji, and it has already been recorded from the Ellice Group by Schmeltz. It is shown in this Museum from New Guinea.

STROMBUS GIBBERULUS, *Linne.*

Tryon, *loc. cit.*, p. 121, pl. viii., fig. 85.

Only seen in a dead state on the beach of the Funafuti lagoon.

Cuming found this at the Society Islands. Tryon gives it from New Guinea, Fiji, and the Paumotus; and Melvill and Standen from Lifu. It is in this Museum from Torres Straits, Louisiades, and New Hebrides.

---

* Martens—Journ. Linn. Soc., Zool., xxi., 1889, p. 189.
† Schmeltz—Mus. Godeffroy, Cat. v., 1874, p. 112.
‡ Schmeltz—*Loc. cit.*, p. 142.

STROMBUS SAMAR, *Dillwyn.*

Tryon, *loc. cit.*, p. 121, pl. viii., fig. 88.

Mr. G. Sweet procured one specimen.

STROMBUS LUHUANUS, *Linne.*

Tryon, *loc. cit.*, p. 122, pl. viii., figs. 91, 92.

Abundant alive on sandy patches between rocks in the lagoon of Funafuti. The natives call it "paneia" and esteem it as food.

Tryon quotes it from New Guinea and Fiji, and Melvill and Standen from Lifu. It extends along the Australian coast south to Sydney.*

PTEROCERA AURANTIA, *Lamarck.*

Tryon, *loc. cit.*, p. 124, pl. ix., fig. 5.

One imperfect but recognisable specimen from Funafuti.

Schmeltz quotes this from Samoa and the Carolines.† It is in this Museum from Fiji.

PTEROCERA BYRONIA, *Gmelin.*
(Fig. 18).

Tryon, *loc. cit.*, p. 124.

A native guided me to the haunt of this mollusc, a gravel flat on the western side of the lagoon, on which the water was waist-deep at low tide. Here I collected numerous living examples. All the older specimens, though alive, had lost the fingers of the shell, which disfigured them almost beyond specific recognition. (Fig. 18). Mr. Whitelegge has pointed out to me that the callous lining of the aperture is everywhere perforated by some vegetable organisms, probably algæ. He suggests that their action has resulted in these mutilations.

On the opercula of most specimens were seated a couple of *Hipponyx australis,* Quoy.

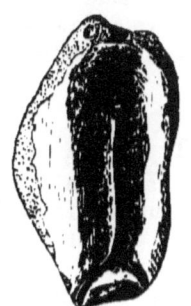

Fig. 18.

The natives, who termed it "karea," valued it for food both raw and roasted, and in ancient times used it as an edge for various implements. By mistake, I have referred to this species in preceding pages (pp. 67 and 263) as *P. lambis.*

Cuming collected this species in the Society islands, the Chevert Expedition in Torres Straits, and specimens have been received by this Museum from Erromanga, New Hebrides.

---

* Hedley—Proc. Linn. Soc N.S.W., xxi., 1896, p. 88.
† Schmeltz—Mus. Godeffroy Cat. v., 1874, p. 141.

PTEROCERA RUGOSA, *Sowerby*.

Tryon, *loc. cit.*, p. 126, pl. x., fig. 12.

I saw a living specimen in the hands of another member of our party, and picked up a dead shell on the beach.

Cuming found this at the Society Islands. New Caledonian examples are contained in this Museum.

TEREBELLUM SUBULATUM, *Lamarck*.

Tryon, *loc. cit*, p. 131, pl. xi., figs. 27 – 30.

Only twice seen, and that in a dead state, on the shore of the Funafuti lagoon.

Schmeltz records this from Samoa, Fiji, and the Pelews. The Chevert Expedition took it in Torres Straits. Melvill and Standen cite it from Lifu. In this Museum it is from the Bampton Reef and Aneitoum, New Hebrides. I have also taken it at Port Moresby, British New Guinea, and Noumea, New Caledonia.

CERITHIUM NODULOSUM, *Bruguière*.

Tryon, *loc .cit.*, ix., 1887, p. 122, pl. xix., figs. 13, 14; pl. xx., fig. 15.

A small form, only 70 mm. or so in length, was not uncommon alive at low water mark on the reefs in the lagoon. This species was observed in Torres Straits by the "Chevert" Expedition.

CERITHIUM COLUMNA, *Sowerby*.

Tryon, *loc. cit.*, p. 123, pl. xx., figs. 17 – 20.

Frequent on the lagoon beach. It is represented in this Museum from Moreton Bay, Queensland, New Caledonia, Fanning Island and Hawaii. Smith reports it from San Christoval, Solomons, Schmeltz from Samoa and the Paumotus, and Melvill and Standen from the Loyalties; it was taken in Fiji by the "Challenger," and in Torres Straits by the "Chevert" Expeditions.

CERITHIUM CITRINUM, *Sowerby*.

Tryon, *loc. cit.*, p. 123, pl. xx., figs. 21 – 23.

Three specimens of a dwarf form, only 7 mm. long, from the lagoon beach are referred to this species. Already recorded from the Ellice by Schmeltz.

CERITHIUM ECHINATUM, *Lamarck*.

Tryon, *loc. cit.*, p. 123, pl. xx., figs. 25 – 27.

One example. Hugh Cuming collected this at Anaa, Paumotus.

CERITHIUM MACULOSUM, *Mighels.*

Kobelt, Conch. Cab., "Cerithium," 1895, p. 499, pl. xxxv., figs. 18, 19.

One dead shell from the lagoon beach. Also occurs at Hawaii.

CERITHIUM ROSTRATUM, *Sowerby.*

Tryon, *op. cit.*, p. 130, pl. xxiii., figs. 90, 91.

Three specimens from the lagoon beach. There are examples in this Museum from the New Hebrides; Pease observed it in Hawaii; Hugh Cuming at Marutea, Paumotus; Brazier at San Christoval, Solomons; the "Chevert" took it in Torres Straits, and Tryon gives it from Fiji.

CERITHIUM OCEANICUM, sp. nov.
(Fig. 19).

Shell rather elongate, almost truncate anteriorly. Colour uniform chocolate. Whorls eight, the upper biangulate, the last equal in length to the remainder. Sculpture: there are on the penultimate whorl (including varices) twenty low, rounded, longitudinal ribs, which crenulate the suture. These cross regularly from whorl to whorl, becoming fewer but proportionately stronger as they ascend the spire; on the last whorl they become evanescent. Two spiral lines of granules descend the spire, appearing on the crest of each rib as a smooth boss. On the body whorl there are besides, beneath these, three spiral lines in which the beads have nearly fused into a smooth continuous ridge, the uppermost of these is sometimes apparent in the spire as a super sutural fasciole. The whole surface of the shell except the beads, is covered by close, microscopic, raised spiral hair lines. Three, obliquely ascending, continuous lines of varices mount the spire a third of a whorl apart. Aperture slightly oblique, semilunate; anterior canal hardly more than a notch, directed sideways; columella anteriorly truncated, externally wrinkled and curved downwards and outwards, internally with a low ridge-tubercle, callus on body whorl medium; outer lip strongly variced behind, edge sharp, notched by the major spiral sculpture, finely grooved within. Length 8, breadth 4 mm.

Fig. 19.

A single, perhaps not quite adult specimen from the lagoon beach.

This shell seems to be a dwarf of the species which Sowerby has figured* as "*Cerithium granosus*, Kiener." The shell which Kiener himself figures† so differs in contour, sculpture, size,

---

* Sowerby—Thesaurus Conch. ii., 1855, pl. clxxxi., fig. 123, 124.
† Kiener—Coquilles Vivantes, Canaliferes i. (n.d.), pl. iv., fig. 5, p. 57.

colour and details of the aperture, that Sowerby's determination can only be considered as one of the blunders which so plentifully occur in his works.

CERITHIUM BREVE, var. ELLICENSIS, var. nov.
(Fig. 20).

Shell conical, blunt in front and tapering somewhat rapidly behind. Colour cream. Apex of the only example broken, remaining whorls seven, of which the upper are much eroded. Sculptured by low rounded longitudinal ribs which crenulate the suture and project at the periphery, on the antipenultimate there are thirteen of these, on the penultimate fifteen, and on the last whorl where they tend to disappear, there are counting varices, eleven. The last whorl is girdled by six, the earlier by two zones of raised and polished callus, which swell into greater prominence on the crest of each rib. The space between these zones is scored by sharp, narrow, revolving grooves, widest apart in the centre.

Behind the aperture is a broad outstanding varix which ascends the penultimate whorl to the lower callus zone. Half a whorl further back is another but much weaker varix. No varices can certainly be distinguished on the spire, though some slightly more prominent ribs there suggest them. Aperture perpendicular, oval, anterior canal short, oblique and deeply cut; inner lip with a heavy layer of callus terminating above and below in a ridge tubercle. Anteriorly and externally the columella is reflected, not appressed to the shell. Outer lip within much thickened, armed with seven entering ridges of callus. Length 10, breadth 5 mm.

Fig. 20.

One specimen from the lagoon beach, differs from type by smaller size and less prominent sculpture.

Of the figures accessible to me, this form most resembles those of *C. hanleyi*, Sowerby, and *C. rubrolineatum*, Sowerby,[*] from which it seems to differ by smaller size, absence of coloured bands, and apparently different arrangement of the teeth of the aperture. Tryon unites these two, and comments severely on this author's nomenclature. Sowerby himself, by a negligence truly remarkable, omits both from his later Monograph in the Conchologia Iconica. The original figure of *C. breve*[†] seems to be badly drawn. As Kiener had access to the original specimens of Quoy and Gaimard, I would rather base an identification on his different but well drawn figure.[‡] Smith has suggested[§] that "*C. breve* may be

[*] Sowerby—Thesaurus Conch. ii., 1855, pl. clxxxiii., figs. 193 and 199.
[†] Voy. "Astrolabe," Zool., 1835, pl. liv, fig. 9.
[‡] Kiener—*Loc. cit.*, pl. xiv., fig. 2.
[§] Smith—Mollusca, Zool. Coll. "Alert," 1884, p. 65.

only a form of *C. morus*, Lamk." Tryon, ever ready to reduce synonymy, agreed in this view. Whatever may be deemed the value of *C. breve*, it cannot be adjudged an absolute synonym of *C. morus*.

The type of *C. breve* came from Tongatabu. The shell does not seem to have been again observed.

CERITHIUM SPICULUM, sp. nov.
(Fig. 21).

Shell narrow, subulate, with a sharply-pointed spire and a rounded base. Colour dull white, distantly, faintly, irregularly, and minutely spotted with chestnut. Whorls eleven, slowly increasing, somewhat turreted, flattened. Sculpture—on the uppermost whorls the spiral ridges are tuberculated by longitudinal plications which rapidly diminish as the growth proceeds. On the last whorl their influence is barely perceptible in faint, shallow, longitudinal undulations. A stout varix occurs a third of a whorl behind the aperture ; from four to ten, raised, spiral cords encircle each whorl, in the interstices of which are fine spiral threads. Aperture perpendicular, oval ; outer lip straight and sharp ; canal very short, turned abruptly outwards. Length 11, breadth 4 mm.

Fig. 21.

Two specimens were obtained in the outer beach of Nukulailai.

This form appears allied to *C. lacteum*, Kiener,* from which it differs by smaller size, narrower outline, and absence of granulations.

CERITHIUM STRICTUM, sp. nov.
(Fig. 22).

Shell narrow, elongate, tapering in a slender spire and blunt anteriorly. Colour white, irregularly longitudinally splashed with chestnut. Whorls seven, the upper angled, the last straight. Sculpture—round the angle of the upper whorls runs a line of tubercles, of which eleven occur on the penultimate. Very slight longitudinal undulations, hardly to be called ribs, extend from these tubercles across the whorl ; both vanish before attaining the last whorl. This latter is girt with about twenty, sharp, revolving ridges, of which the central is largest and corresponds to the tuberculated angle of the earlier whorls ; the rest vary in size and spacing, the basal ridges being least and closest ; the upper seven ascend the spire. A large varix is behind the aperture, and a

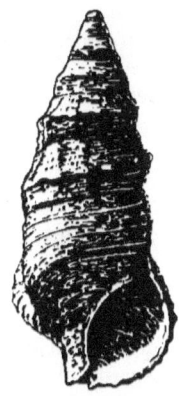

Fig. 22.

* Kiener—Coquilles Vivantes, Canaliferes i., (n.d.), p. 58, pl. vii., figs. 3, 3a.

Dd

weaker one half a whorl back, none else appear. Aperture perpendicular, oval. Outer lip smooth within, sharp edged, crenulate
outside, inner lip excavate, thickly lined with callus, with a
posterior nodule at the margin of the channelled angle. Length
7, breadth 3 mm.

A single specimen from the lagoon beach.

This species seems related to *C. maculosum*, Mighels ; it is far
more slender, and differs in that the revolving line of tubercles
fails to attain the last whorl.

CERITHIUM VARIEGATUM, Quoy & Gaimard.

Tryon, *loc. cit.*, p. 134, pl. xxiv., figs. 41, 43, 45, 65, 66.

Some imperfect examples collected by Mr. Sweet are with
hesitation so determined.

CERITHIUM ZEBRUM, Kiener.

Tryon, *loc. cit.*, p. 137, pl. xxv., figs. 71, 72.

I refer to this species a small shell abundant on the lagoon beach,
7 mm. long, variously coloured—brown, cream, mauve and salmon,
unbanded and banded. No really satisfactory figure or description
of it exists, the earliest is much the best. Melvill and Standen, who
recognise it from the Loyalties, erroneously state that it was originally described from the Galapagos, whence Sowerby reported it.
The locality given by Kiener himself* is Mauritius. Tryon adds
Samoa. I found it in Port Moresby, British New Guinea and at
Oubatche, New Caledonia. It is represented in this Museum
from the New Hebrides. So widespread and variable a species
probably possesses a synonomy to match. I agree with Langkavel's†
remark that *C. ianthinum* of Gould, should be here included,
which would extend the geographical range of the species to
Tahiti and the Paumotus. It is likely that *C. unilineatum*, Pease
and *C. dichroum*, Melvill and Standen should be reduced to *C.
zebrum*. Pease adds *C. aspersum*, Deshayes as a synonym.‡

CERITHIUM IMPENDENS, sp. nov.
(Fig. 23).

Shell strong, stout, regularly conical, each of the upper whorls
overhanging the next, bi-angled above the suture, heavily
variced on the back of the last whorl. Colour — upon a
white ground is painted ochre-yellow, in one instance chocolate,
which chiefly prevails on the base and between the ribs, thus
accentuating the projections to the eye. Whorls eight, suture
deeply impressed. Sculpture—peculiar buttress ribs ornament the

---

* Kiener—Coquilles Vivantes, Canaliferes i., (n.d.), p, 72.
† Langkavel—Donum Bismarckianum, 1871, p. 25.
‡ Pease—Am. Journ. Conch. vii., 1872, p. 75.

spire, the penultimate whorl has ten and those above a proportionate decrease; they are weak at the suture, which they barely sinuate, and gain in breadth and height as they cross the whorl, projecting over the suture beneath them. They do not cross continuously from whorl to whorl, nor do they regularly alternate; they grow evanescent on the last whorl and cease with a stout and heavy varix one-third of the whorl behind the aperture. In this latter space, reminiscences of them occur as tubercles on the angle and at the suture. On the last whorl about twenty fine spiral threads are evenly distributed between the suture and the

Fig. 23.

anterior point of the shell; the uppermost of these ascend the spire and are alike prominent on ribs and interspaces. Aperture perpendicular, subtriangular; columella sharply sinuate, anterior notch not produced into a canal; callus on body whorl slight; outer lip thickened slightly and reflected, angled sharply at the posterior insertion. Length 4½, breadth 2 mm.

Seven examples from the lagoon beach. Perhaps this is a member of the subgenus *Colina*.

CERITHIUM PIPERITUM, *Sowerby*.

Tryon, *loc. cit.*, p. 144, pl. xxvii., figs. 31, 32.

Mr. G. Sweet procured a few dead shells of this species at Funafuti. It had previously been recorded from the Ellice by Schmeltz, and also from Upolu and Rarotonga. There are examples from Tahiti in this Museum.

CERITHIUM OBELISCUS, *Bruguière*.

Tryon, *loc. cit.*, p. 146, pl. xxvii., fig. 39.

One specimen from the lagoon beach. Melvill and Standen report this from the Loyalties; Schmeltz from Fiji and Cook's Islands; and Smith from Tonga.* In this Museum it is represented from Cooktown and Port Curtis, Queensland, also New Caledonia, Lord Howe Island and Hawaii.

CERITHIUM OBELISCUS, var. CEDO-NULLI, *Sowerby*.

Tryon is here followed in reducing this to varietal rank. In Funafuti it is represented by an extremely small and stout individual, 22 mm. long. First found at Anaa, Paumotus.

CERITHIUM ASPERUM, *Linne*.

Tryon, *loc. cit.*, p. 148, pl. xxviii., figs. 62, 63.

One of the commonest shells on the lagoon beach; the lineated form dominant. It was taken by the "Chevert" in Torres Straits,

---

* Smith—Proc. Zool. Soc., 1891, p. 416.

by the "Challenger" at Fiji and Tonga, and under the synonym of
C. lineatum, Lk., is reported by Melvill and Standen from the
Loyalties; and by Schmeltz from Cook's Islands.

CERITHIUM PHAROS, *Hinds.*

Tryon, *loc. cit.*, p. 149, pl. xxix., fig. 68.

Mr. G. Sweet brought one specimen from Funafuti. Tryon reports this from Fiji and the Paumotus. In this Museum it is
represented from New Caledonia, New Hebrides, and Hawaii.

CERITHIUM ELEGANTISSIMUM, sp. nov.

(Fig. 24).

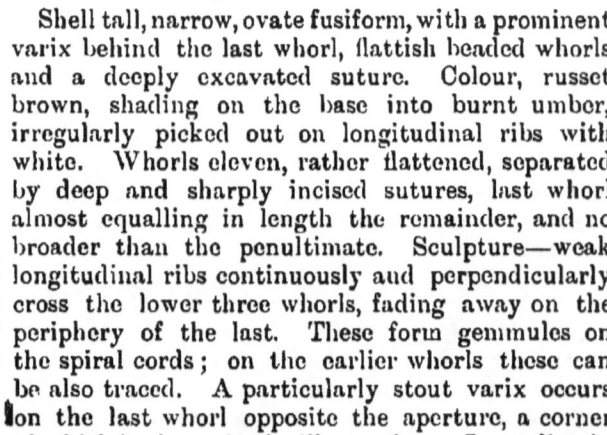

Shell tall, narrow, ovate fusiform, with a prominent
varix behind the last whorl, flattish beaded whorls
and a deeply excavated suture. Colour, russet
brown, shading on the base into burnt umber,
irregularly picked out on longitudinal ribs with
white. Whorls eleven, rather flattened, separated
by deep and sharply incised sutures, last whorl
almost equalling in length the remainder, and no
broader than the penultimate. Sculpture—weak
longitudinal ribs continuously and perpendicularly
cross the lower three whorls, fading away on the
periphery of the last. These form gemmules on
the spiral cords; on the earlier whorls these can
be also traced. A particularly stout varix occurs
on the last whorl opposite the aperture, a corner
of which is shown in the illustration. Immediately
beneath the suture winds a slender cord; four spiral rows of
gemmules encircle the space between it and the periphery, the
uppermost of which tends to split into two; the remaining space
between the periphery and the anterior extremity is occupied by
seven simple cords which become more slender and close anteriorly;
the upper whorls have but two beaded cords. The aperture is
perpendicular and oval, strongly variced without and consequently
shelved within; columella arched, with a thick brown callus;
canal very short and wide, slightly recurved. Length 5, breadth
2 mm.

Fig. 24.

Abundant on stones in shallow water in the lagoon at Funafuti.

A specimen before me from Thursday Island, Queensland,
differs slightly from the above in the greater prominence of the
longitudinal ribbing.

CONTUMAX, gen. nov.

A genus of the Cerithiidæ, nearest allied to *Cerithiopsis*. It
shares with that the excavated base, the produced canal, and the
unfinished aperture; but differs by greater size, broader shell,

more rapidly increasing whorls, different plan of sculpture, and especially by a habit of plugging and breaking off the upper whorls from time to time. Animal unknown.

Type.—*C. decollatus*, Hedley.

The genus is founded on a species from Funafuti. I have also a cogeneric but apparently distinct species from Oubatche, New Caledonia, which is 15 mm. long ; white, with a few scattered brown dots ; without the longitudinal plications of the Funafuti species, but rather more distinctly cancellated by longitudinal sculpture. I am also disposed to include under *Contumax* the species which Melvill and Standen describe* as *Mathilda eurytima*, whose "canali producto" so ill agrees with *Mathilda*. Perhaps this *M. eurytima* may be the young of the Oubatche shell just mentioned. The genus is also represented from Torres Straits.

CONTUMAX DECOLLATUS, sp. nov.

(Fig. 25).

Shell narrow, conical, above rounded, below turreted, solid, invariably decollated. Colour, dull white. Whorls of an uncertain number, the specimen figured has seven, and I estimate that five more have been lost. Sculpture—the shell has three stages, which merge into each other, but which apart might seem to belong to different species. None of a fairly large series before me show the apical whorls, the summit being in every instance and in successive stages broken off. The youngest whorl before me is rounded and crossed by several fine raised spiral lines. Later the median line enlarges and originates an angle, and a faint longitudinal sculpture appears. Further on, the whorl is sharply angled by a strong keel, below which are two minor keels, and on the shelf above are five delicate spiral lines, all of which are more or less beaded by transverse sculpture. On the antepenultimate whorl commence longitudinal plications which

Fig. 25.

rapidly develop to their maximum on the last whorl. Here they are six in number, oblique, commencing at the suture, most prominent on the shoulder and vanishing at the basal keel.

The base is hollow, overhung by a thick basal ridge, within which is a second lesser one, the remainder of the base being faintly concentrically striated. Aperture scarcely oblique, squarish,

---

* Melvill & Standen—Journ. Conch. viii., 1896, p. 310, pl. xi., fig. 73.

lip simple, sharp, columella arched, canal produced and recurved. Length 18, breadth 8 mm.

Several dead specimens collected on the lagoon beach of Funafuti.

CERITHIOPSIS EUTRAPELA, *Melvill & Standen.*

Melvill & Standen, Journ. Conch., viii., 1896, p. 301, pl. x, fig. 52.

Three specimens, one mauve, the others white, from the lagoon beach of Funafuti.

CERITHIOPSIS ELECTRINA, sp. nov.

(Fig. 26).

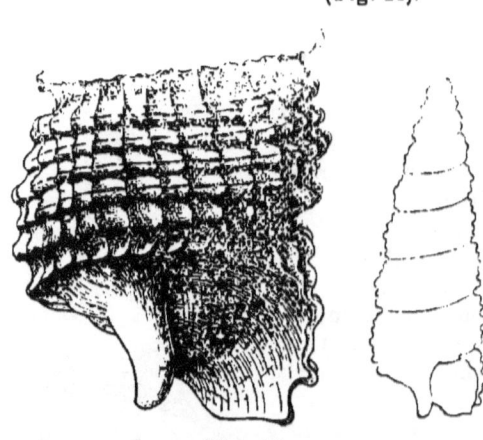

Fig. 26.

Shell tall, slender, thin and translucent. Colour uniform pale amber, except a glassy white topmost whorl. Whorls nine in my example, whose tip is broken. Sculpture— on the earlier whorls proportionately fewer, on the last, six spiral alternately larger and smaller rows of crowded gemmules, which also regularly succeed one another in longitudinal order, being continued across the suture from whorl to whorl and ascending the spire obliquely. The individual gemmules, as seen in profile are much elevated, seen in full face are oval; those of the upper four rows of the last whorl are impressed and bisected by a shallow transverse groove, invisible in profile, but apparently doubling the transverse rows of gemmules when seen in full face. Above the first and below the fifth row, the longitudinal axis of each continues as a pillar, giving a fluted aspect to the broad and deep sutural excavation. The lowest row is swallowed by the suture of the subsequent whorl. Beneath the sixth row the shell is much undercut and then tapers to the columella. The aperture is nearly square with sharp outer lip, arched columella, and very short perpendicular canal. Length 4½, breadth 1½ mm.

One specimen from the lagoon beach of Funafuti.

This appears to be distinguished from other Pacific *Cerithiopsis* by the more numerous rows of closely packed granules.

TRIFORIS DOLICHA, *Watson.*

Watson, Chall. Report, Zool., xv., 1886, p. 565, pl. xlii., fig. 1.

One specimen from the Funafuti lagoon agrees exactly with another now before me from Prince of Wales Island, Torres Straits. Young specimens were collected off Cape Sidmouth, Queensland, by Mr. A. U. Henn, and presented to this Museum. The "Challenger" collected it a little west of Cape York.

The two adult specimens I have seen are pure white, punctuated between the gemmules with orange; in neither is the lip more developed than in the "Challenger" example. It may be that this species does not attain the spurred lip of its congeners.

TRIFORIS ÆGLE, *Jousseaume.*
(Fig. 27)

Jousseaume, Bull. Soc. Mal. France, 1884, p. 256, pl. iv., fig. 12 ;
Tryon, Man. Conch., ix., 1887, p. 185, pl. xxxix., fig. 40.

Fig. 27.

Jousseaume's account, as reflected in Tryon's Manual is too scanty to allow of a proper determination, and with much doubt I assign here a Funafuti species. A single specimen of *T. ægle,* from Noumea, presented by Mr. R. C. Rossiter, now before me, is too immature to show the aperture. It is a larger and lighter coloured shell than those from Funafuti, and the gemmules seem rather closer together. As, however, it fairly corresponds to the Ellice shells in apex and sculpture, I prefer, instead of adding another name to the long list of *Triforis,* to assume that the one figured and described below is a variety of Jousseaume's species. The still more scanty information published relative to *T. collaris,* Hinds, suggests that it should also be compared.

___

* Hinds—Proc. Zool. Soc., 1843, p. 23 ; and Journ. Conch., viii., 1897, p. 409.

Shell rather narrow, tapering to a fine and slender point. Whorls fifteen. Colour ochraceous with white gemmules. Protoconch six whorled, first two together semiglobose and shagreened ; remainder keeled by a single, strong, central, projecting carina, which is beaded by the passage of numerous close set delicate bars crossing the whorls obliquely. All adult whorls except the last have two rows of gemmules, about sixteen in a row, alternating vertically. On the last whorl there are two additional anterior rows of smaller gemmules, an incipient row on the periphery and two minor scarcely beaded ridges on the base. The gemmules are large and very prominent, polished and reflecting a nacreous lustre, rounded anteriorly, flattened with corner angles peripherally and shelved atop ; each is linked to its neighbours in the row by a coloured ridge ; in the centre of the whorl a sharp groove runs between the two rows. The surface in general is decussated by faint growth lines crossing spiral engraved lines. Aperture nearly perpendicular, ovate, inner lip with a thick callus layer, outer lip thickened and reflected, the right margin crossing the canal in a spur ; anal notch cordate, the orifice taking the place of the last sutural gemmule, canal oblique, moderately produced. Length 5, breadth $1\frac{1}{4}$ mm.

Shallow water in the lagoon. The commonest *Triforis* at Funafuti.

Prominent characters which distinguish this species are the large, white, facetted, gemmules contrasted against the dark background, the one-keeled apex, and the peculiar anal notch.

TRIFORIS TORQUATUS, sp. nov.

(Fig. 28).

Shell moderately broad. Whorls fifteen, suture sharply impressed. Colour orange buff ; on the ninth and tenth whorls the lower rows of gemmules are chocolate, and on the last row two narrow bands of chocolate cover two anterior rows of gemmules, stain the lip and wind down the throat ; on the eleventh, twelfth, thirteenth and fourteenth whorls, the lower lines of gemmules are white ; the seventh and eighth whorls are entirely white. Protoconch six whorled, first two together semiglobose, remainder keeled by a single, strong, central, projecting carina, which is beaded by coarse, slightly oblique bars. All adult whorls, except the last, have two rows of gemmules, about seventeen to a row, alternating vertically. On the last whorl there is in addition a peripheral and two basal ridges, all scarcely beaded. On the penultimate whorl a thread appears in the space between the gemmules, and follows the sinuations of the upper tier as far as the aperture without gaining equal rank. The gemmules are polished hemispherical bosses, shelved above, distant about half

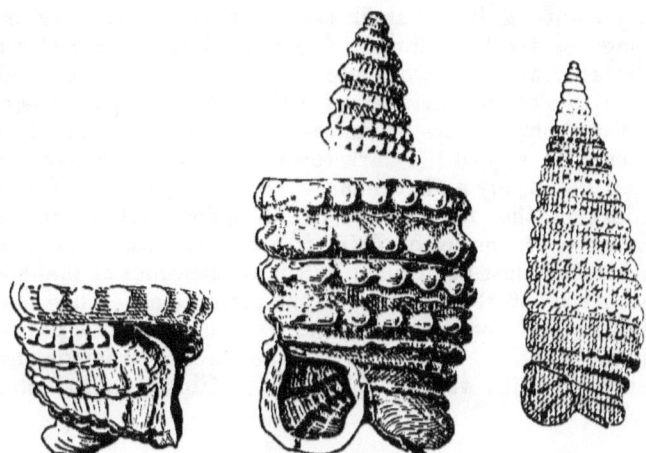

Fig. 28.

their own diameter from their neighbours in a row, and linked to them by an inconspicuous raised coloured ridge. Between the gemmules the surface is microscopically shagreened and finely spirally grooved. The aperture is perpendicular, and nearly square; outer lip thickened and reflected, the right margin crossing the canal in a spur; anal notch deep; semicircular canal short, blunt, oblique. Length 5, breadth 2 mm.

Several specimens alive in the Funafuti lagoon.

The peculiar colouration of this species facilitates recognition. Even the unaided eye can detect the two chocolate lines on the base and spire, and the white spiral band ascending the intermediate whorls. This colour scheme I have endeavoured to convey in Fig. 28.

In colour *T. cinguliferus*, Pease, appears to resemble *torquatus*, but the figure given by Langkavel, copied and coloured by Tryon, represents a stouter shell with a different aperture.

The group *(Mastonia*, according to Tryon) to which this belongs, might be conveniently divided into two sections, having a one-keeled and a two-keeled protoconch, respectively. The present species with *T. dolicha* and *T. ægle* would belong to the former.

I have collected *T. torquatus* also at Port Moresby, British New Guinea.

TRIFORIS RUBER, *Hinds.*

(Fig. 29).

Hinds, Ann. Mag. Nat. Hist., xi., 1843, p. 18.

The species before me is the most abundant, conspicuous and widespread of the genus in the tropical Pacific. If I have

correctly identified it, the shell was first taken by Belcher during
the voyage of the "Sulphur." He noticed it at Port Carteret,
New Ireland, as "numerous among fine gravel at low water."
There are two colour varieties of this shell—one pale, the other
dark. Conchological tradition appears universally, but I think
erroneously, to regard the dark form as *T. ruber* and the pale as
T. violaceus of Quoy and Gaimard. For the purpose of specific
determination the descriptions of all older writers, and most
modern ones, of species of *Triforis* are worthless. The identity
of *T. violaceus* must be decided by the illustrations of that species
in the "Atlas of the Voyage of the Astrolabe." This shows a
slender and produced anterior canal, and an anal notch projecting
as a complete tube, remote from the aperture. Specimens answering to these details, which I collected in Milne Bay, British New

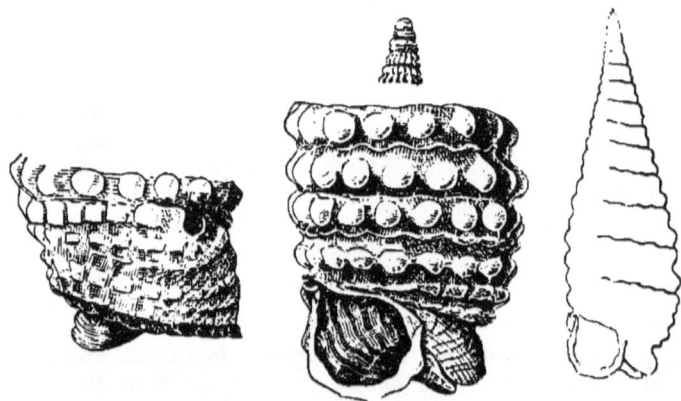

Fig. 29.

Guinea, are before me. Though Quoy and Gaimard may them-
selves have confounded distinct species, and though Kiener's
figure from "Astrolabe" material appears to disagree with the
former illustration, yet the only safe point of departure in un-
ravelling the nomenclature of this group must be Figs. 22 and 23
of Pl. lv. of the Atlas aforesaid. In the particulars of the anal
and anterior orifices, the shell before me, presumed to be *T. ruber*,
differs altogether, as the accompanying drawings show.

In the unsatisfactory state of literature, the following remarks
may not be deemed superfluous.

This species varies in size, stoutness, and colour; from the
adult an immature shell so differs in outline, that a collector does
not at first recognise it as the same kind, for it much resembles
Triforis gemmulatus, Adams and Reeve.* As a whole the contour
of the adult shell resembles that of a carrot, the upper whorls

* Adams & Reeve—Zool. Samarang, 1850, Mollusca, pl. xi., fig. 34 *a, b.*

tapering to a slender point, the lower swollen to bulbous. Colour, which alters in drying, reddish purple to lilac, the apex and the lower row of gemmules usually cream. Whorls about eighteen. Gemmules subcircular, polished bosses, shelved above, separated by about half their own diameter, in two rows of about twenty-two in a whorl, alternating vertically ; the interspaces between the gemmules are spirally wrinkled. On the antipenultimate whorl a spiral thread arises between the two rows of gemmules, but following the sinuations of the upper, this gradually increases, becomes segmented, and on the last whorl forms an additional row of gemmules. Just behind the aperture extra rows are also intercalated. The protoconch is acicular, four or five whorled, the whorls bicarinate, crossed obliquely by numerous fine bars, which bead the carinæ. The aperture is perpendicular, almost square, lip reflected, the right margin crossing the canal in a spur, the canal being closed by its anterior wall folded over, but not touching the pillar. Anal notch deep, a subcircular, subtubular, orifice in the place of the last sutural gemmule ; onwards from the last actual gemmule the lip is free from the body whorl. Length $7\frac{1}{2}$ mm.

Common in shallow water in the lagoon of Funafuti. As the rare *T. violaceus* has been generally confounded with the common *T. ruber*, whose aperture is quite different, most literary records are untrustworthy, and I forbear to quote them. I have myself collected the species at Port Moresby and Milne Bay, British New Guinea, and at Oubatche and Noumea, New Caledonia. Specimens of *T. ducosensis*, Jousseaume, received from Noumea, from Mr. R. C. Rossiter, belong to the pale form of *T. ruber*.

TRIFORIS CLIO, sp. nov.

(Fig. 30).

Shell rather small and slender. Colour cinnamon-brown, lowest row of gemmules and extremity of canal white, other gemmules pale brown. Whorls fifteen. Protoconch five whorled ; first two together swollen and subglobose, shagreened, remainder bicarinate by a median furrow and crossed by numerous fine bars which bead the carinæ. The adult whorls are beset by first two, then three, and finally four spiral rows of gemmules, eighteen to a whorl, set vertically, gemmule above gemmule, up the spire. Broad furrows ascend vertically from whorl to whorl, deeper than the spiral interspaces which part row from row. The gemmules are lozenge shaped, polished, standing half their length apart and linked to their neighbours in a row by a coloured band smoother and shallower than the remainder of the vertical furrow, of which it forms a part. Between the gemmules the surface is roughened by close fine spiral hair lines. Two unbeaded cords run round the base. Aperture nearly vertical, outer lip bending round a

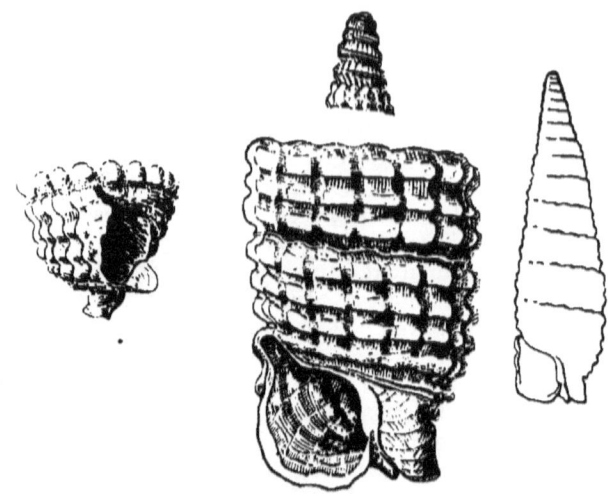

Fig. 30.

shallow rounded anal notch, then deeply emarginate and finally much produced, crossing the pillar in a spur. Canal short and rather sharply recurved. Length $5\frac{1}{2}$, breadth $1\frac{3}{4}$ mm.

Three examples were found in shallow water in the Funafuti lagoon. The most mature, depicted here, is possibly not quite adult and the anal notch may attain a further development.

The lozenge shaped gemmules and the exceptional feature of the longitudinal furrows being deeper than the transverse assist in distinguishing the species.

TRIFORIS OBESULA, *Jousseaume*.

(Fig. 31).

Jousseaume, Bull. Soc. Mal. France, 1884, p. 255, pl. iv. fig. 17 ;
    Tryon, Man. Conch., ix., 1887, p. 185, pl. xxxviii., fig. 27.

Jousseaume's account of this species is not accessible to me and I have to assume that Tryon gives a faithful transcript of it. That however only allows me to identify the shell I now figure and describe as *T. obesula*, with probability rather than certainty. My perplexity is increased by the fact that the Funafuti shell is identical with specimens received from New Caledonia labelled "*T. limosa*, Jousseaume," with the description of which they disagree in shape and size.

The species is distinguished by its small size, corpulent shape and dark brown (burnt umber) hue. The type of sculpture differs from that of the other species of *Triforis* from Funafuti. The gemmules are so closely packed within the row and are so feebly divided from one another, that they seem rather to be a continuous keel, like that of *T. corrugatus*, in process of breaking down into beads. The earlier adult whorls are ornamented by two bead-rows. Between them there arises in the antipenultimate a thread, which gradually increasing becomes a full grown row in the last whorl ; the addition of a median and two basal rows brings the number of rows on the last whorl to six. Tryon states that the "three anterior ones are unarmed," but all are beaded in the example before me.

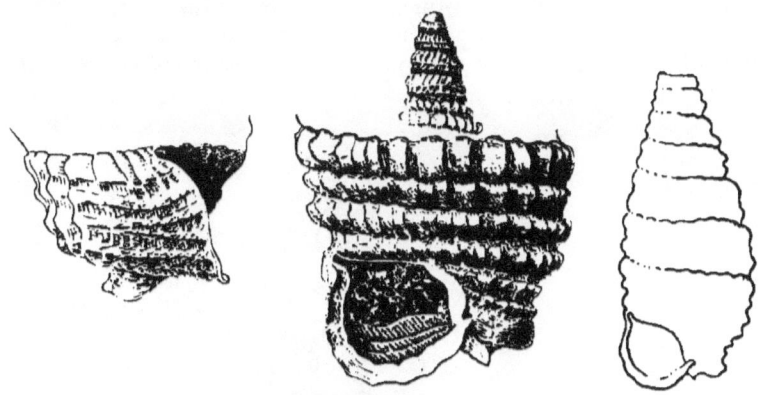

Fig. 31.

The anal notch is simple and comparatively shallow. The protoconch has five whorls, the first hemispherical and smooth, the others bicarinate and obliquely crossed by rather coarse bars which do not bead the carinac. The adult sculpture suddenly commences in the sixth whorl with a row of small beads above and a large gemmed ridge below. The latter is remarkable in several specimens before me for its white colour, giving the shell to the unaided vision a distinct white collar beneath the acicular apex. Tryon gives the length as 8 mm. Of the examples before me the New Caledonian measure $4\frac{1}{2}$, the Papuan 4, and the decollated shells from Funafuti $3\frac{1}{2}$ mm.

Two decollated specimens occurred to me in the Funafuti lagoon. I have also taken the species between tide marks in Port Moresby, British New Guinea. A Papuan specimen supplied the material for the above account of the apex, missing in Funafuti and New Caledonian examples.

TRIFORIS THETIS, sp. nov.
(Fig. 32).

Shell small and slender. Colour uniform cinnamon-brown except a patch of dark chocolate on the columella. Whorls fifteen. Protoconch five whorled, the later three bicarinate, crossed obliquely by numerous fine bars which bead the carinæ. The adult whorls are beset with two bead-ridges, carrying each about sixteen gemmules of equal size to a whorl, vertically the gemmules run slightly oblique, between each ridge is a deep and narrow groove. In the antepenultimate whorl a thread appears in this groove and ultimately grows on the last whorl to a gemmule row. A raised thread beneath the suture ascends for a few whorls. The last whorl is ornamented by this thread followed by a row of large gemmules, two rows of smaller ones, an incipient peripheral row and two minor, basal, subnodulose ridges. The gemmules are coloured, polished, hemispherical, truncated and shelved above, and stand nearly their diameter apart on the ridge.

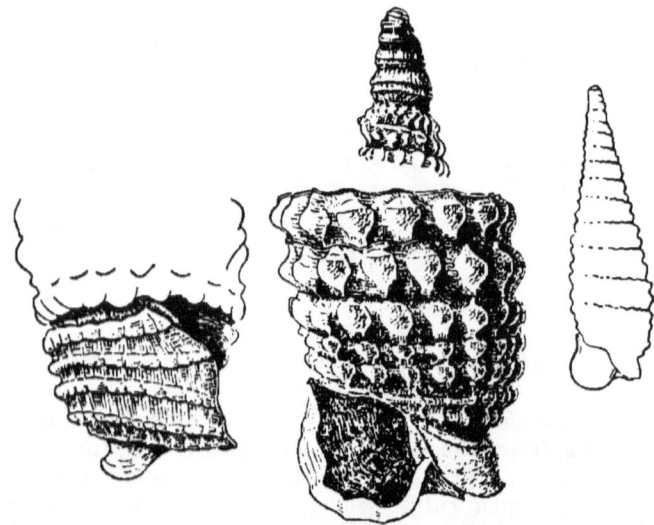

Fig. 32.

The suture is deep and well defined. Between the gemmules the surface is roughened by minute spiral threads cut by oblique growth lines. Aperture vertical, nearly square. Outer lip crossing the pillar in a spur. Anal notch a simple open fold. Canal short and briefly recurved. Length 4, breadth 1 mm.

Shallow water in the Funafuti lagoon, several specimens.

Seeing that Tryon, whose standard of description was not severe, concludes his monograph of the genus with a list of eighty unrecognizable *Triforis*, I have no confidence that the species above described has not previously appeared in literature, though I am sure that it has never been properly characterised. It is probably near, and possibly identical with, *T. limosa*, Jousseaume. That writer (as repeated by Tryon) neglects the important details of apex, anal notch, etc., and the fact that the Funafuti shells are but half its size, has decided me, in the absence of other information to regard it as distinct. A shell from Port Moresby closely resembles the Ellice one, differing by larger size and more swollen contour.

TRIFORIS INCISUS, Pease.
(Fig. 33).

Tryon, <i>loc. cit.</i>, p. 190, pl. xxxix., fig. 65.

The inadequate description and poor figure quoted, suggest, but fail to demonstrate, that a shell figured herewith should be so named. The species is represented by a single, perforated and decollated example from the Funafuti lagoon. It is $5\frac{1}{2}$ mm. in length, has thirteen whorls remaining, and in colour is ochraceous splashed with white. The last whorl has six spiral ridges, two of which are basal; the three preceding whorls have each three, and those above each two such ridges. The ridges are smooth, elevate and keeled, the anterior of each series the larger; on the upper

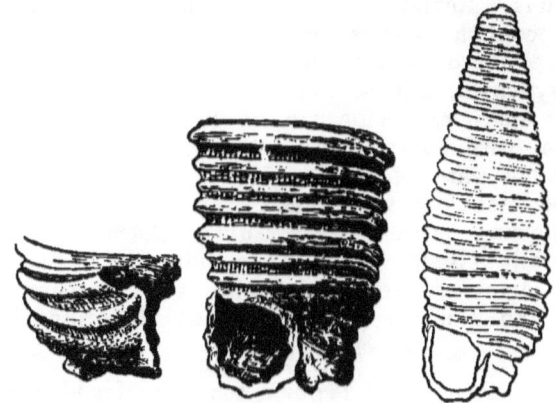

Fig. 33.

whorls the posterior ridge tends to divide into beads. The interstices are broad, deep and finely spirally grooved. The spur of the outer lip crosses the pillar. Anal notch deep and cordate. Canal short and perpendicular.

Pease described <i>T. incisus</i> from Hawaii.* I have collected at Port Moresby, British New Guinea, what seems a form of that described above. It differs in colour being variegated with black, chocolate and white. The uppermost ridge has not the same disposition to become beaded but longitudinal plications are developed in the interstices. The protoconch in these Papuan shells is six whorled, bicarinate and crossed by coarse bars, like the apex I figure for <i>T. obesula</i>.

---

* Pease—Proc. Zool. Soc., 1860, p. 434.

TRIFORIS CORRUGATUS, *Hinds.*

Hinds, Ann. Mag. Nat. Hist , xi., 1843, p. 18; Hinds, Voy. "Sulphur,"
Zool., pl. viii., fig. 12 ; Chenu., Man. Conch , 1859, p. 284, figs.
1915, 1916 ; Langkavel, Donum Bismarckianum, 1871, p. 26,
pl. ii., fig. 6 ; Tryon, Man. Conch., ix., 1887, p. 189, pl.
xxxix., fig. 59.

T. connatum, Montrouzier, Journ. Conch., x., 1862, p. 236, pl.
ix., fig. 4.

A considerable series of specimens from various localities and a
careful examination of the literature quoted, enable me to confidently unite Montrouzier's species with that of Hinds.   It should
be obvious to any student who compares the excellent figure in
the Journal de Conchyliologie with the other illustrations that
the immaturity of the New Caledonian example is the only point
of difference.   That this synonymy of so common and distinct a
species should have so long escaped attention is another sad proof
of the negligence of the authors who have dealt with this much
abused genus.   Reviewing the shells of Lifu, Melvill and Standen
actually record the species first under one name and then under
the other.*   Tryon has suggested *T. bayani*, Jousseaume, as a
probable synonym, an idea which his figures seem to contradict.
One of the specimens before me shows the protoconch to have a
double keel, with a very narrow interstice.

The shallow water of the Funafuti lagoon yielded me several
broken specimens.   A wide range over the Pacific is indicated
by the following records :—New Guinea (Belcher) ; Queensland,
Torres Straits, (Brazier)† and Cape Sidmouth, (Henn); Gilbert
Islands (Garrett) ; New Caledonia, Ile Art (Montrouzier) ;
Oubatche and Noumea (Hedley) ; and Lifu (Hadfield).

TRIFORIS, spp.

Several other species of *Triforis*, too worn for identification or
determination are included in the collection.

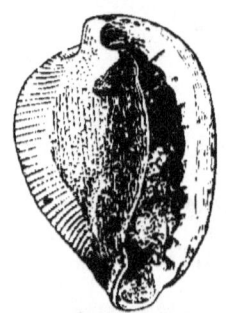

OVULA HERVIERI, sp. nov.
(Fig 34).

Shell small, broadly ovate.   Colour pale
yellow with four spiral bands of rose, visible
alike within the aperture, across the callus
and on the dorsal surface, these bands are in
breadth equal to their interstices. Sculpture—
about thirty-five flat-topped spiral lyræ, separated by narrow, sharply incised grooves,
surround the shell.   The outer lip is much
thickened and reflected without, and bears
within about ten slight and widely parted

Fig. 34.

* Melvill & Standen, *loc. cit.*, viii., pp. 114 and 409.
† Brazier—Proc. Linn. Soc. N.S.W., i., 1876, p. 319.

denticules. The callus on the inner lip is very heavy, its surface shagreened, posteriorly it rises into an abrupt boss and anteriorly is heaped in a longitudinal ridge. Length 4, breadth 3 mm.

Taken alive from the deep water Gorgonidæ raised from the western slope of Funafuti in eighty to forty fathoms.

This very distinct little species, the smallest of its genus known, appears to find its nearest relation in *Ovula caledonica*, Crosse;* from which it is easily separated by smaller size, greater proportional breadth, coarser sculpture and fewer labial denticules.

It is named in compliment to the Rev. J. Hervier, the author of many clear descriptions and admirable drawings of Pacific shells.

CYPÆA ARGUS, *Linne.*

Tryon, Man. Conch., vii., 1885, p. 164, pl. i., figs. 1, 2 ; Garrett, Journ. Conch., ii., 1879, pp. 106, 109.

Dead shells were found on the beach of one of the western islets of Funafuti, and the species was again encountered at Nukulailai.

According to Garrett, this deep water species inhabits the Carolines, Gilberts, Tonga, Fiji and Samoa. Rossiter records it from New Caledonia, the Isle of Pines and the Loyalties.† From material in this Museum I add the Solomons, Erromanga and Aneiteum, New Hebrides.

CYPRÆA SCURRA, *Chemnitz.*

Tryon, *loc. cit.*, p. 165, pl. ii., figs. 19, 20, 21 ; Garrett, *loc. cit.*, pp. 107, 118.

One dead shell was taken on Funafuti.

Tryon quotes it from Anaa, Paumotus. Garrett found this in Fiji, Tonga, Samoa, Gilberts, Carolines, Cook's, Society, Paumotus, Marquesas, and Hawaii. A series in this Museum include instances from the Gilberts, the Louisiades, Woodlark Island, New Caledonia and Broken Bay, N. S. Wales.

CYPRÆA TESTUDINARIA, *Linne.*

Tryon, *loc. cit.*, p. 165, pl. i., figs. 9, 10 ; Garrett, *loc. cit.*, pp. 107, 119.

Mr. G. Sweet procured an example of this on Funafuti.

Garrett, enumerates this from Fiji, Tonga, Samoa, Gilberts, Carolines, Cook's and Society. Tryon mentions it from New Caledonia. In this Museum it is shown from Niue, the Solomons and Erromanga, New Hebrides.

---

* Crosse—Journ. de Conch., xx., 1872, p. 62, pl. ii., fig. 1.
† Rossiter—Proc. Linn. Soc. N.S.W., vi., 1882, p. 817.

Ee

CYPRÆA ISABELLA, *Linne.*

Tryon, *loc. cit.*, p. 165, pl. i., figs. 6, 7; Garrett, *loc. cit.*, pp. 106, 114.

Dead shells were plentiful on the Funafuti beach.

The range through Polynesia as given by Garrett, is the same as that of *C. scurra.* The collection of this Museum shows the species to occur along the Australian coast south to the Bellenger River, N.S. Wales, and in the Central Pacific from Niue, Woodlark Island, British New Guinea, Erromanga, and Aneiteum, New Hebrides, New Caledonia and the Gilberts to Hawaii.

CYPRÆA CARNEOLA, *Linne.*

Tryon, *loc. cit.*, p. 166, pl. iii., figs. 26 – 30 ; Garrett, *loc. cit.*, pp. 106, 110.

Though I saw none alive, dead specimens were plentiful on the beach of the Funafuti lagoon.

Found by Garrett to accompany the foregoing through the ten archipelagoes enumerated ; and seen by Rossiter from New Caledonia, Loyalty Islands, and Isle of Pines.

This species ranges along the Australian coast south to Sydney. Specimens in this Museum show it from the Solomons.

C. CARNEOLA, var. PROPINQUA, *Garrett.*

Garrett, Journ. Conch., ii., 1879, p. 116.

Two specimens are referable to this variety, which is also represented in the Australian Museum from Niue, the Society and Gilbert Groups. Garrett records it from the Paumotus.

CYPRÆA TALPA, *Linne.*

Tryon, *loc. cit.*, p. 167, pl. iii., figs. 31 – 33 ; Garrett, *loc. cit.*, pp. 107, 119.

' One empty shell was found at Funafuti with *C. argus.*

Garrett collected this deep-water species at Fiji, Tonga, Samoa, Gilberts, Carolines, Cook's, Society, Paumotus, and Hawaii. It is shown in this Museum to occur in British New Guinea, the Solomons, Erromanga, New Hebrides, New Caledonia, and Niue.

CYPRÆA GOODALLI, *Gray.*

Tryon, *loc. cit.*, p. 168, pl. iv., figs. 43, 44 ; Garrett, *loc. cit.*, pp. 106.

Mr. G. Sweet found one well preserved example at Funafuti. Garrett only knew this from Cook's, Society, and Paumotus. There are specimens in this Museum from the Gilberts.

CYPRÆA FIMBRIATA, *Gmelin.*

Tryon, *loc. cit.*, p. 168, pl. v., figs. 76 – 78 ; Garrett, *loc. cit.*, pp. 106, 112.

Dead shells were noticed at Funafuti and at Nukulailai.

Garrett observed this from the same Groups as *C. talpa*. This species ranges along the Australian coast south to Sydney. Museum specimens include it from Milne Bay, British New Guinea, New Caledonia, Niue, the Gilberts, and Hawaii. Tryon quotes it from the Paumotus.

Cypræa macula, *Adams.*

Tryon, *loc. cit.*, p. 169, pl. iv., figs. 71, 72.

Mr. G. Sweet obtained one specimen.

Cypræa mauritiana, *Linne.*

Tryon, *loc. cit.*, p. 173, pl. vii., figs. 8 – 11.

Specimens of this were purchased from the natives of Funafuti.

Collected by Garrett at Fiji, Tonga, Samoa, Gilberts, Carolines, Cook's, Society, Paumotus, Marquesas, and Hawaii, and by Rossiter in New Caledonia and the Loyalties. Weinkauff mentions it from the Pelew Islands. I have seen it from the British and German Boundary, N.E. New Guinea. In this Museum it is also represented from Aneiteum and Erromanga, New Hebrides, and Niue.

Cypræa caput-serpentis, *Linne.*

Tryon, *loc. cit.*, p. 173, pl. vi., figs. 98 – 100, xxiii., fig. 59; Garrett, *loc. cit.*, pp. 106, 111.

Commonly found alive under stones in shallow water in the Funafuti lagoon.

Seen by Garrett in Fiji, Tonga, Samoa, Gilberts, Carolines, Cooks, Society, Paumotus and Marquesas. This extends along the Australian coast south to Sydney, and is also represented in this Museum from Erromanga, New Caledonia, Lord Howe Island, Niue, and the Gilberts. The natives of Funafuti call this " pourei."

Cypræa mappa, *Linne.*

Tryon, *loc. cit.*, p. 174, pl. vii., figs. 12 – 14; pl. viii., fig. 17; Garrett, *loc. cit.*, pp. 106, 115.

Mr. G. Sweet procured one dead specimen of this. ·

According to Garrett the range embraces Fiji, Tonga, Samoa, Gilberts, Carolines, Cook's, Society, and Paumotus. It is in this Museum from the Louisiades. Tryon quotes New Caledonia.

Cypræa arabica, *Linne.*

Tryon, *loc. cit.*, p. 174, pl. viii., figs. 18, 19, 23, 24; Garrett, *loc. cit.*, pp. 106, 108.

Occasionally found alive under coral blocks in the Funafuti lagoon.

Garrett noticed this in Fiji, Tonga, Samoa, Gilberts, Carolines, Society and Paumotus. Brazier* has remarked it from Torres Straits southwards to Botany Bay, from Fiji, New Britain, New Ireland, New Caledonia and the Solomons. It is further represented in this Museum from Woodlark Island (British New Guinea), Erromanga and Aneiteum (New Hebrides), and Niue.

CYPRÆA RETICULATA, *Martyn*.

Tryon, *loc. cit.*, p. 174, pl. viii., figs. 20 – 22 ; Garrett, *loc. cit.*, pp. 107, 117.

A small variety occurs alive in the Funafuti lagoon.

Garrett saw this in the Gilberts, Cooks, Society, Paumotus, Marquesas and Hawaii.

CYPRÆA MONETA, *Linne*.

Tryon, *loc. cit.*, p. 177, pl. x., fig. 46; pl. xi., figs. 51 – 54; pl. xxiii., figs. 60 – 69 ; Garrett, *loc. cit.*, pp. 106, 115.

Abundant alive under stones round the margin of the Funafuti lagoon.

Garrett records it from Fiji, Tonga, Samoa, Carolines, Cook's, Society, Paumotus, Marquesas, and Hawaii. This species ranges along the Australian coast from Torres Straits south to Sydney.† I have seen it at Milne Bay and Port Moresby, British New Guinea. In this Museum are examples from Niue, Teste Island, Louisiades, the Solomons, Erromanga, New Hebrides, New Caledonia, and Lord Howe Island. "At Eramanga," writes Brenchley,‡ " a shell called '*Nunpuri*,' the *Cypræa moneta*, passes as money, as also in New Caledonia."

CYPRÆA MONETA, var. ANNULUS, *Linne*.

Occurred as usual in company with the species in chief, with which, like *C. obvelata*, and contrary to the opinion of monographers, it intergrades by easy stages.

CYPRÆA TIGRIS, *Linne*.

Tryon, *loc. cit.*, p. 180, pl. xi., figs. 49, 50; pl. xv., fig. 8; Garrett, *loc. cit.*, pp. 107, 120.

I picked up one broken shell on the beach of Funafuti, and purchased a specimen from a native on Nukulailai.

Seen by Garrett from Fiji, Tonga, Samoa, Gilberts, Carolines, Cook's, Society, Paumotus, Marquesas, and Hawaii. This occurs

* Brazier—Journ. Conch. ii., 1879, p. 194.
† Henn—Proc. Linn. Soc. N.S.W. (2), x., 1895, p. 520.
‡ Brenchley—The Cruise of the " Curaçoa," 1873, p. 299.

along the Australian coast as far south as Moreton Bay.* Melvill and Standen name it from Lifu. In this Museum it is shown from Woodlark Island, Solomons, and Erromanga, New Hebrides. I have seen it at Port Moresby, British New Guinea, where the natives call it " nononono."

CYPRÆA VITELLUS, *Linne.*

Tryon, *loc. cit.*, p. 182, pl. xiii., figs. 72, 73 ; Garrett, *loc. cit.*, pp. 106, 121.

One specimen was obtained at Funafuti by Mr. Sweet.

Garrett took this species at Fiji, Tonga, Samoa, Gilberts, Carolines, Cook's, Society, Paumotus, Marquesas, and Hawaii. It ranges along the Australian coast south to Sydney. Further instances from Niue, the Louisiades, New Caledonia, and Erromanga, are supplied by this Museum.

CYPRÆA LYNX, *Linne.*

Tryon, *loc. cit.*, p. 183, pl. xiv., figs. 86, 87, 98 ; Garrett, *loc. cit.*, pp. 106, 114.

Found alive under stones in the Funafuti lagoon.

Except the Marquesas, this species, says Garrett, ranges all through Polynesia. It inhabits the Australian coast south to Moreton Bay. The collection of this Museum exhibits it from Erromanga, New Hebrides, New Caledonia, Fiji, and the Gilberts.

CYPRÆA CLANDESTINA, var. ARTUFFELI, *Jousseaume.*

Melvill & Standen, Journ. Conch., viii., 1896, p. 112, pl. iii., figs. 28, 29.

Alive in the lagoon of Funafuti. Previously reported from Lifu.

CYPRÆA CRIBRARIA, *Linne.*

Tryon, *loc. cit.*, p. 190, pl. xvii., figs. 71, 72.

I did not find this species, which has been recorded from the Ellice by Schmeltz.

CYPRÆA EROSA, *Linne.*

Tryon, *loc. cit.*, p. 192, pl. xviii., figs. 1, 90, 100; Garrett, *loc. cit.*, pp. 106, 111.

Mr. G. Sweet brought a specimen from Funafuti. Garrett observed that, except at the Marquesas, it was not uncommon at all the groups he visited. It ranges along the Australian coast south to Broken Bay. A specimen from Erromanga, New Hebrides, is now before me.

---

* Brazier—Proc. Linn. Soc. N.S.W., v., 1881, p. 501.

CYPRÆA PORARIA, *Linne.*

Tryon, *loc. cit.*, p. 193, pl. xviii., figs. 2, 3 ; Garrett, *loc. cit.*, pp. 107, 116.

A few dead shells were obtained from the beaches of Funafuti.

Garrett obtained this at Fiji, Tonga, Samoa, Gilberts, Carolines, Cook's, Society, Paumotus, and Hawaii. Rossiter records it from New Caledonia and the Loyalty Islands.

CYPRÆA HELVOLA, *Linne.*

Tryon, *loc. cit.*, p. 194, pl. xix., figs. 8, 9 ; Garrett, *loc. cit.*, pp. 106, 113.

I found one alive under a coral boulder on the western side of the Funafuti lagoon.

Garrett collected this at Fiji, Tonga, Samoa, Gilberts, Carolines, Cook's, Society, Paumotus, Marquesas, and Hawaii. Rossiter gives it from New Caledonia, Loyalty, and Isle of Pines. This extends south along the Australian coast as far as Sydney.

CYPRÆA CICERCULA, *Linne.*

Tryon, *loc. cit.*, p. 197, pl. xx., figs. 55 - 58, 61, 62 ; Garrett, *loc. cit.*, pp. 107, 122.

Several empty shells from the beach drift of Funafuti.

Noted by Garrett from Fiji, Tonga, Samoa, Gilberts, Carolines, Cook's, Society, Paumotus, and Hawaii; and by Rossiter from New Caledonia and the Loyalty. In this Museum it is also shown from Niue, Torres Straits, and Aneiteum, New Hebrides.

CYPRÆA NUCLEUS, *Linne.*

Tryon, *loc. cit.*, p. 197, pl. xx., figs. 48, 49 ; Garrett, *loc. cit.*, pp. 107, 125.

Frequently seen dead on the Funafuti beach.

Observed by Garrett at Fiji, Tonga, Samoa, Gilberts, Carolines, Cook's, Society, Paumotus, and Hawaii. Rossiter reports it from the Loyalty. There are specimens in this Museum from the Solomons and New Hebrides.

CYPRÆA CHILDRENI, *Gray.*

Tryon, *loc. cit.*, p. 198, pl. xx., figs. 53, 54 ; Garrett, *loc. cit.*, pp. 107, 122.

Mr. G. Sweet found one of this at Funafuti.

Garrett reports it from Fiji, Tonga, Samoa, Gilberts, Cook's, Society, and Paumotus. Specimens from New Caledonia, Niue, and Hawaii are in this Museum.

TRIVIA ORYZA, *Lamarck*.

Tryon, *loc. cit.*, p. 200, pl. xxi., figs. 79, 82, 83 ; Garrett, *loc. cit.*, pp. 107, 126.

Several dead specimens of a small form of this species were collected on the beach of the Funafuti lagoon.

This ranges along the Australian coast as far south as Sydney. Garrett remarks that this has the same range and station in Polynesia as the preceding species. Rossiter notes it from Noumea, New Caledonia, and the Loyalty. It is shown in this Museum from the New Hebrides.

DOLIUM PERDIX, *Linne*.

Tryon, *loc. cit.*, p. 264, pl. iii., fig. 15 ; pl. iv., figs. 23 – 25.

I was unable to obtain an example of this circumæquatorial species on Funafuti, but I identified one purchased from a native by another member of our party.

Melvill and Standen note this from Lifu. This Museum has representatives from British New Guinea, the Solomons, Erromanga, New Hebrides, New Caledonia, the Gilberts, and Niue.

DOLIUM POMUM, *Linne*.

Tryon, *loc. cit.*, p. 265, pl. v., fig. 26.

One specimen from the lagoon beach.

Tryon quotes this from the Society Islands. Material in this Museum indicates it from British New Guinea, New Caledonia, and the Gilberts.

CASSIS CORNUTA, *Linne*.

Tryon, *loc. cit.*, p. 270, pl. i., figs. 45, 46 ; pl. ii., fig. 49.

I collected no examples of this personally, but at Funafuti I remarked it in use as shell trumpets, and at Nukulailai I purchased specimens. There the natives called it " pou," and told me it was not rare. New Caledonian examples are contained in this Museum.

CASSIS VIBEX, var. ERINACEA, *Linne*.

Tryon, *loc. cit.*, p. 277, pl. vii., fig. 90.

Two dead shells from the lagoon beach.

TRITONIUM TRITONIS, *Linne*.

Tryon, Man. Conch., iii., 1881, p. 9, pl. i., fig. 1 ; pl. iii., fig. 16 ; pl. iv., fig. 25.

I did not myself collect this species. Mr. J. O'Brien told me that it was sometimes found on the leeward reefs alive. The natives recognised an engraving of it as " bofala."

TRITONIUM PILEARE, *Linne*.

Tryon, *loc. cit.*, p. 12, pl. vi., figs. 31 - 36; pl. vii., figs. 38, 39.

A few were found alive in the lagoon. Tryon indicates the range of this species as circumæquatorial. Its occurrence in every archipelago in the Pacific is therefore to be expected.

TRITONIUM CHLOROSTOMUM, *Lamarck*.

Tryon, *loc. cit.*, p. 13, pl. vii., figs. 47, 48.

One empty shell from the lagoon beach of Funafuti. This species appears to share the geographical range of its predecessor.

TRITONIUM GEMMATUM, *Reeve*.

Tryon, *loc. cit.*, p. 13, pl. vii., figs. 41 - 44.

A single specimen was taken on Funafuti.

Tryon cites this from the Paumotus, and Melvill and Standen from Lifu. Representatives from New Caledonia and Fanning Island are in this Museum.

TRITONIUM DIGITALE, *Reeve*.

Tryon, *loc. cit.*, p. 29, pl. xv., figs. 142, 143.

Common alive in the Funafuti lagoon.

Tryon gives Fiji, and Smith* Strong Island, as localities. In this Museum it is exhibited from San Christoval, Solomons, Aneiteum, New Hebrides, Marquesas, and Hawaii.

TRITONIUM TUBEROSUM, *Lamarck*.

Tryon, *loc. cit.*, p. 23, pl. xiii., figs. 111 - 113.

One specimen, alive, from the Funafuti lagoon.

From Lifu, Melvill and Standen note this species; and examples from Woodlark Island and Port Moresby, British New Guinea, repose in this Museum.

TRITONIUM MACULOSUM, *Gmelin*.

Tryon, *loc. cit.*, p. 25, pl. xiv., fig. 121.

One dead shell was found on a western islet of Funafuti. This Museum has the species from the Gilberts.

DISTORTRIX ANUS, *Linne*.

Tryon, *loc. cit.*, p. 35, pl. xv., fig. 153 ; pl. xvii., figs. 173, 174.

I did not find this species on Funafuti, but have seen specimens collected there by Mr. G. Sweet.

---

* Smith—Journ. Linn. Soc., Zool., xii., 1876, p. 551.

Tryon mentions it from the Society Islands. Examples from the Solomons are contained in this Museum.

GYRINEUM BUFONIUM, *Gmelin.*

Tryon, *loc. cit.*, p. 39, pl. xxi., figs. 21 - 23, 28, 29, 68 ; pl. xix., fig. 11 ; pl. xx., figs. 13, 14.

Several were found alive under stones in shallow water in the Funafuti lagoon.

Inhabits the Paumotus, according to Tryon, and is shown in this Museum from Torres Straits, Solomons, and New Caledonia.

GYRINEUM AFFINE, *Broderip.*

Tryon, *loc. cit.*, p. 42, pl. xxii., figs. 38 - 41 ; pl. xxiii., fig. 55.

An empty shell was found on the lagoon beach of Funafuti.

Tryon notes it from New Caledonia, Samoa, and Paumotus. *G. graniferum*, Lamarck, has been recorded from the Ellice by Schmeltz.

PERISTERNIA NASSATULA, *Lamarck.*

Tryon, *loc. cit.*, p. 80, pl. lxiv., figs. 44 – 47, 51, 52, 58.

Abundant in the rock-pools of the outer reef of Funafuti.

Tryon quotes this from New Guinea, New Caledonia, and the Paumotus ; and Schmeltz from Upolu and Rarotonga.

LATIRUS POLYGONUS, var. BARCLAYI, *Reeve.*

Tryon, *loc. cit.*, p. 88, pl. lxvii., fig. 110.

A few dead shells from the beach of the Funafuti lagoon.

Schmeltz records this from Fiji.

LATIRUS CRATICULATUS, *Linne.*

Tryon, *loc. cit.*, p. 93, pl. lxix., fig. 159.

Not common ; a few dead shells seen on the lagoon beach of Funafuti.

Schmeltz mentions it from Upolu and Rarotonga. Specimens from New Caledonia are in this Museum.

PISANIA FASCICULATA, *Reeve.*

Tryon, *loc. cit.*, p. 146, pl. lxxi., figs. 195, 197.

Recorded by Schmeltz from the Ellice.

CANTHARUS UNDOSUS, *Linne.*

Tryon, *loc. cit.*, p. 162, pl. lxxiv., figs. 280 - 282.

Living specimens were taken in the lagoon of Funafuti.

Represented in this Museum from Port Curtis, Queensland, and New Caledonia.

MUREX ADUSTUS, *Lamarck*.

Tryon, Man. Conch., ii., 1880, p. 90, pl. xv., figs. 148, 149; pl. xxiv., figs. 210 – 212; pl. xxv., fig. 217.

Common in shallow water in the lagoon of Funafuti.

Noted from Lifu by Melvill and Standen, and represented in this Museum from New Caledonia.

MUREX FUNAFUTIENSIS, sp. nov.

(Fig. 35).

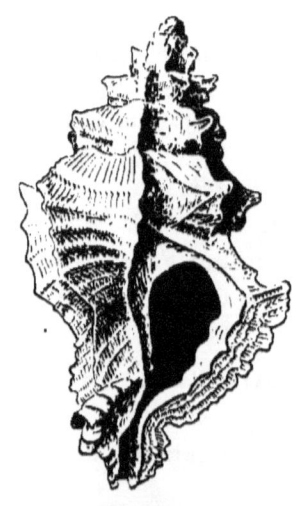

Fig. 35.

Shell small, biconical. Colour ochraceous buff, banded with chocolate, interior of aperture pale lilac. Whorls seven, sculptured each with seven prominent varices, which mount the spire continuously and obliquely. On the spire each varix presents a hollow spine above a blunt tubercle. Between and parallel to the varices are a series of imbricating lamellæ. Five spiral ridges run round the shoulder of the shell, and undulate both the blades and the interstices of the varices. The lamellæ are likewise microscopically beaded by minute spiral threads. The aperture is oblique, ovate, choked by an inner tuberculate ridge, and by the great development of the columella; the latter is arched, deeply obliquely entering, anteriorly with two incipient tubercles, and truncate below. Canal short, open, and recurved; above it are two series of disused canals, corresponding to the ultimate and penultimate varices. Length 9, breadth 5 mm.

One specimen, taken by tangles, at a depth of forty to eighty fathoms, on the western slope of Funafuti.

This species approaches nearest to *Murex nuclea*, Reeve,* which it resembles both in colour and form. Judging from his account of that species, it differs by being just half the size, by having seven whorls instead of five, with seven varices apiece instead of six, and especially by being longer in proportion to breadth than the Philippine shell is. Whether these differences are constant or not I cannot say.

---

* Reeve—Conch. Icon. iii., 1845, Murex, pl. xxix., sp. 131.

MUREX RADULA, sp. nov.

(Fig. 36).

Shell small, fusiform. Colour cream, spines orange, columella pale lilac. Whorls seven. Sculpture—eight feeble varices alternating on each whorl. On the third and fourth whorls they are proportionately much stronger and are angled at the periphery. The body whorl has eleven spiral cords, narrower than their interstices; both are overridden by fine lamellæ in the line of growth. At frequent intervals these cords produce small, short, tubular, orange spines, which lend a conspicuous and recognizable aspect to the shell. Apex of three whorls conical, smooth, and glossy. Aperture simple, lip sharp, canal broad and open. Length 9, breadth 4 mm.

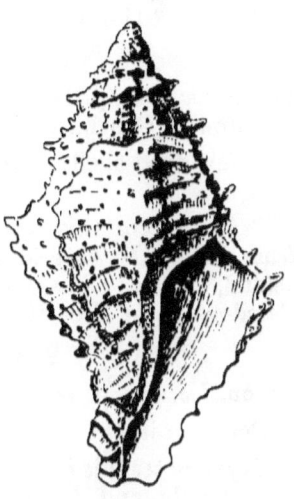

Fig. 36.

A single specimen, taken at a depth of forty to eighty fathoms with the preceding. This specimen is perhaps immature, but differs so much from any with which I am acquainted as to be considered worthy of description.

PURPURA HIPPOCASTANEUM, *Lamarck.*

Tryon, *loc. cit.,* p. 162, pl. xlv., figs. 36 – 43 ; pl. xlvi., fig. 45.

Abundant on the outer reef of Funafuti. Tryon quotes this from the Paumotus, and Melvill and Standen from the Loyalty. In this Museum are instances from Queensland, Fiji, and the Solomons. Both Cooke* and Smith† condemn the treatment of the species in the reference quoted above, but, unfortunately for puzzled students, both think it "needless to discuss the matter at length."

The species seems to me to stand nearer *Sistrum* than *Purpura.* The natives called this " matapoto."

PURPURA ARMIGERA, *Chemnitz.*

Tryon, *loc. cit.,* p. 163, pl. xlvi., figs, 50, 51.

Abundant on the outer reef of Funafuti, where its massive shell enables it to withstand the heaviest surf. In aged specimens the projecting points are worn down to the stump.

---

* Cooke—Journ. Conch., v., 1888, p. 323.
† Smith—Proc. Zool. Soc., 1891, p. 408.

Tryon quotes this from the Paumotus, and Schmeltz from Bowen (Queensland). It is in this Museum from New Caledonia and British New Guinea.

JOPAS SERTUM, *Bruguière.*

Tryon, *loc. cit.*, p. 180, pl. lv., figs. 181, 188‒190 ; Pease, Am. Journ. Conch., iv., 1868, p, 117.

A few dead shells were collected on the beach of the Funafuti lagoon.

Tryon quotes this from the Paumotus ; Melvill and Standen from Lifu. In this Museum it is represented from Woodlark Island, British New Guinea, the Solomons, Santa Cruz, New Caledonia, and Hawaii.

SISTRUM HYSTRIX, *Linne.*

Tryon, *loc. cit.*, p. 183, pl. lvi., fig. 195.

Common in the rock pools of the outer reef of Funafuti.

Tryon notes this from Hawaii, Fiji, and Paumotus, and Schmeltz from Upolu and Rarotonga. It is in this Museum from New Caledonia.

SISTRUM HORRIDUM, *Lamarck.*

Tryon, *loc. cit*, p. 184, pl. lvi., figs. 201, 202.

Abundant in the rock pools of the outer reef of Funafuti.

Tryon mentions this from Hawaii, and Melvill and Standen from the Loyalty. It is in this Museum from Samoa.

SISTRUM RICINUS, *Linne.*

Tryon, *loc. cit.*, p. 184, pl. lvi., fig. 200 ; pl. lvii., figs. 204, 206, 212.

Abundant in the rock pools of the outer reef of Funafuti.

Melvill and Standen record this from Lifu. Specimens from Woodlark Island, British New Guinea, and Hawaii, are included in this Museum.

SISTRUM MORUS, *Lamarck.*

Tryon, *loc. cit.*, p. 185, pl. lvii., figs. 213, 214.

One specimen from the Funafuti lagoon.

In this Museum from the New Hebrides, New Caledonia, Lord Howe Island, Niue, and Tahiti.

SISTRUM DIGITATUM, *Lamarck.*

Tryon, *loc. cit.*, p. 185, pl. lvi., fig. 191 ; pl. lvii., fig. 203.

Occurred with the preceding, but uncommon.

Melvill and Standen enumerate this from Lifu. It is represented in this Museum from Woodlark Island and New Caledonia.

SISTRUM TUBERCULATUM, *Blainville.*

Tryon, *loc. cit.*, p. 186, pl. lvii., figs. 218, 220.

Abundant in rock pools on the outer reef of Funafuti.

According to Tryon this inhabits Hawaii. Schmeltz mentions Rockhampton (Queensland), Samoa and Fiji. In this Museum it is shown from New Caledonia and Lord Howe Island.

SISTRUM CANCELLATUM, *Quoy.*

Tryon, *loc. cit.*, p. 188, pl. lviii., figs. 242, 250.

Common in the rock pools of Funafuti.

Tryon mentions this from Hawaii; Schmeltz gives Fiji, Rarotonga, and Tahiti. A specimen from Fanning Island is contained in this Museum.

SISTRUM FISCELLUM, *Chemnitz.*

Tryon, *loc. cit.*, p. 188, pl. lviii., figs. 251 - 257.

Not uncommon on the Funafuti beaches.

Examples from Teste Island, Louisiades, New Caledonia, and Hawaii are preserved in this Museum.

CORALLIOPHILA CORONATA, *Barclay.*

Tryon, *loc. cit.*, p. 210, pl. lxvi., figs. 372, 373.

One worn specimen was gathered on the beach of Funafuti.

Melvill and Standen, who received this from Lifu, were the first to record it from the Pacific.

GALEROPSIS MADREPORARUM, *Sowerby.*

Tryon, *loc. cit.*, p. 212, pl. lxvii., figs. 389 - 391, 398 ; Pease, Am. Journ. Conch. iv., 1868, p. 112. .

Purpura porphyroleuca, Crosse, Journ. de Conch. xix., 1871, p. 322, pl. xiii., fig. 7.

This species was found alive at Funafuti in crevices of living coral, particularly *Millepora.*

Quoy and Gaimard report this from Tonga, Marie from Tahiti, Gould from Wake Island and Samoa, and Melvill and Standen from Lifu. It is also shown in this Museum from New Caledonia, Hawaii, and Vate, New Hebrides.

The description above quoted by Crosse corresponds so well to Sowerby's, that his name may safely be reduced to synonomy.

MAGILUS ANTIQUUS, *Lamarck.*

Tryon, *loc. cit.*, p. 216, pl. lxviii., figs. 400 - 411.

Two young shells were obtained alive in company with the *Galeropsis* just mentioned. Tryon's remark " that all the species that have been differentiated from *M. antiquus* must be regarded with suspicion," has guided my determination. Nothing seems to be recorded of the distribution of this species in the Central Pacific. A specimen from the Solomon Islands is in this Museum.

NASSA SEMITEXTA, sp. nov.

(Fig. 37).

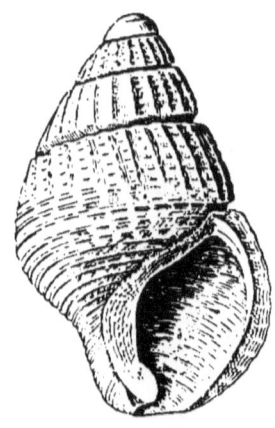

· Shell broadly ovate, small, strong, opaque, white. Whorls five, of which two are apical and smooth. Remainder sculptured by small, regularly spaced, longitudinal ribs; on the last whorl these number twenty-three and vanish below the periphery. Similar spiral ribs, crossing the longitudinals, lattice the upper whorls and the upper third of the last whorl; on the penultimate there are six of these, and on the last whorl about twenty-five, which are strong and widely spaced on the periphery, weak and crowded anteriorly. A deep and narrow groove follows the suture. Aperture oblique, oval, fortified without by a thick and prominent varix, which is crossed by the spiral sculpture; columella arched, spreading a heavy sheet of callus, anteriorly incurved and terminating in a rounded knob; canal open, short, in section C-shaped. Length 6, breadth 4½ mm.

Fig. 37.

A rather worn specimen was found on the lagoon beach by myself, and another was taken by Mr. G. Sweet.

This species is referred to *Nassa* for the unsatisfactory reason that I do not know where else to locate it, and yet the material before me is hardly sufficient foundation for the erection of a new genus. A tubercle near the posterior angle of the aperture is characteristic of *Nassa*, but absent here; while the channelled suture and heavy varix developed here may not be matched in *Nassa*. Indeed, though the contour and anterior notch repel the idea, some aspects of this shell suggest *Rissoina*. Till further data, and the soft parts arrive, the true systematic position of this shell must, I think, remain in suspense.

NASSA GRANIFERA, *Kiener*.

Tryon, Man. Conch., iv., 1882, p. 26, pl. viii., figs. 39 – 41.

Mr. G. Sweet collected one specimen. Melvill and Standen report this from the Loyalty, and the Museum contains it from the New Hebrides.

COLUMBELLA VARIANS, *Sowerby*.

Tryon,. Man. Conch., v., 1883, p. 110, pl. xlv., figs. 1, 2, 97 – 100; pl. xlvi., figs. 3 – 6.

Common alive in the lagoon of Funafuti.

Tryon mentions it from New Guinea, Fiji, Hawaii, and Galapagos. In this Museum it is shown from Niue, Baker's Island and New Caledonia.

COLUMBELLA GALAXIAS, *Reeve.*

Reeve, Conch. Icon., xi., 1859, Columbella, pl. xxxv., sp. 229.

A variable species, plentiful at Funafuti, as also throughout Polynesia, is provisionally so named. This name, though in current use, is probably invalid. Tryon states that the prior name of *C. sagitta,* Gaskoin, belongs here, although Reeve's figure and the original locality are both at variance with the shell in question. This statement has neither been accepted nor denied by London writers ; the latest reference to the species by Melvill and Standen ignores it. We owe the confusion in which this species is involved to the past generation of London Conchologists, and we expect reparation from the present. A perusal of literature suggests that an extensive synonomy will result from a revision of the nomenclature of this species. *Columbella mindorensis,* Reeve, and *C. articulata,* Souverbie, are suggested as probable additions to the names reduced by Tryon.

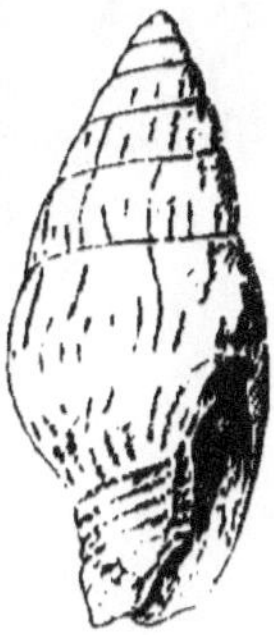

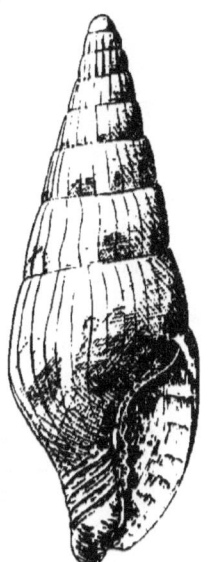

COLUMBELLA MELVILLI, sp. nov.
(Fig. 38).

Shell small, smooth, ovate. Colour white, irregularly longitudinally striped by narrow, brown, broken lines, which are interrupted at the periphery. Whorls seven, slightly rounded, glossy, traversed by a few, scarcely perceptible spiral grooves. Aperture narrow, outer lip straight, simple, not grooved within. Columbella arcuate above, denticulate below. Length $4\frac{1}{2}$, breadth $1\frac{3}{4}$ mm.

Fig. 38.

Rare, alive under stones in the Funafuti lagoon. Named in honour of the senior author of a catalogue of the shells of Lifu, so often quoted in these pages.

COLUMBELLA ALOFA, sp. nov.
(Fig. 39.)

Shell narrow, tall, spire acuminate. Colour cream, with widely spaced, narrow, orange longitudinal lines, and a series of large coral-red blots on the periphery. Whorls eight, the upper three longitudinally finely ribbed and crossed by revolving grooves, the remainder smooth, base sculptured by a few spiral cords. Aperture narrow, outer lip straight, simple, plicate within. Columella dentate, canal slightly recurved. Length 12, breadth 4 mm.

Fig. 39.

One specimen was brought alive from forty to eighty fathoms, on the western slope of Funafuti.

COLUMBELLA OBTUSA, *Sowerby.*

Tryon, *loc. cit.*, p. 181, pl. lix., figs. 59, 60.

Two specimens alive in the Funafuti lagoon.

Tryon quotes this from Fiji, Reeve from Huaheine, and Kobelt from Hawaii. It is in this Museum from the Solomons and the New Hebrides.

COLUMBELLA TRINGA, *Lamarck.*

Tryon, *loc. cit.*, p. 181, pl. lix., figs. 65,66.

One specimen alive in the lagoon.

Tryon mentions this from New Caledonia and Fiji. It is in this Museum from Milne Bay, British New Guinea.

COLUMBELLA RUBICUNDA, *Quoy & Gaim.*

Quoy & Gaim., Voy. "Astrolabe," ii., 1832, p. 588, pl. xl., figs. 25, 26.

Schmeltz* records this from the Ellice, and also *Pyrene aurea,* Lamk.

ENGINA PÁRVA, *Pease.*

Tryon, *loc. cit.*, p. 195, pl. lxiii., fig. 55.

One dead shell on the lagoon beach. Found by Pease in the Paumotus.

ENGINA NODICOSTATA, *Pease*

Tryon, *loc. cit.*, p. 195, pl. lxiii., figs. 56, 57.

One living but immature shell from the lagoon of Funafuti.

Tryon records this species from the Paumotus and Fiji.

ENGINA MENDICARIA, *Linne.*

Tryon, *loc. cit.*, p. 196, pl. lxiii., figs. 62, 73.

Abundant in the rock pools of the outer beach of Funafuti.

Schmeltz names this from Samoa and Fiji, Melvill and Standen from the Loyalty Islands, Kobelt from New Ireland, and Brazier from Torres Straits. Specimens from Port Moresby, British New Guinea, are in this Museum.

MITRA EPISCOPALIS, *Linne.*

Tryon, Man. Conch., iv., 1882, p. 111, pl. xxxii., fig. 1 ; Garrett, Journ. Conch., iii , 1880, pp. 3, 14.

I collected several specimens of this mollusk alive, on sandy gravel flats, in the Funafuti lagoon at low water-mark. The shell

---

* Schmeltz—Cat. Godeffroy Museum, v., 1874, p. 125.

was formerly employed in the manufacture of native implements by the Funafuti people (see *ante* pp. 249, 259) who called it "mouri ounga."

Garrett records this species from the Fiji, Tonga, Samoa, Gilbert, Caroline, Cook, Society, Paumotu, and Hawaiian Groups. Melvill and Standen notice it from the Loyalty.* In this Museum it is also represented from Torres Straits, New Guinea, Solomon Islands, and New Caledonia.

MITRA PONTIFICALIS, *Lamarck.*

Tryon, *loc. cit.*, p. 111, pl. xxxii., fig. 3; Garrett, *loc. cit.*, pp. 4, 23.

Two examples occurred to me in company with the preceding species, and I secured a third at Nukulailai.

Garrett notes for this a range similar to that of *M. episcopalis*, with the addition of the Marquesas. Melvill and Standen publish it from the Loyalty Islands. Examples are in this Museum from Erromanga, New Hebrides, San Christoval, Solomons, and New Caledonia.

MITRA FLAMMEA, *Q. & G.*, var. HYSTRIX, *Montrouzier.*

Montrouzier, Journ. de Conch., x., 1862, p. 241, pl. ix., fig. 8; Tryon, *loc. cit.*, p. 140.

One example from Funafuti is longer and more slender than that described by Montrouzier. Tryon is responsible for the subordination of this form to *M. flammea*.

MITRA CUCUMERINA, *Lamarck.*

Tryon, *loc. cit.*, p. 143, pl. xlii., figs. 227 – 229; Garrett, *loc. cit.*, pp. 3, 14.

Several examples from the rock pools of the ocean beach of Funafuti.

The habitats enumerated by Garrett are : Fiji, Tonga, Samoa, Gilberts, Carolines, Cook's, Society, Paumotus, and Hawaii. Pease records it from the Ralick Islands.† I have taken it at Panie, New Caledonia.

MITRA CHRYSALIS, *Reeve.*

Tryon, *loc. cit.*, p. 144, pl. xlii., fig. 233; Garrett, *loc. cit.*, pp. 3, 13.

Abundant on the outer reef of Funafuti.

Garrett observed this in Fiji, Tonga, Samoa, and the Gilberts. New Caledonian specimens are also before me.

---

* Melvill & Standen—*Loc. cit.*, viii., p. 90.

† Pease—Am. Journ. Conch., iv., 1868, p. 121.

Ff

MITRA TABANULA, *Lk.*, var. CALEDONICA, *Recluz.*

Recluz, Journ. Conch., iv., 1853, p. 248, pl. vii., fig. 7 ; Tryon, *loc. cit.*, p. 146, pl. xlii., fig. 247.

A form represented by four specimens from the outer reef of Funafuti is thus doubtfully determined. It is smaller, smoother, and narrower than the shell figured by Recluz, but approaches nearer to it than to any other illustration.

MITRA FERRUGINEA, *Lamarck.*

Tryon, *loc. cit.*, p. 150, pl. xliv., figs. 279, 280, 290 ; Garrett, *loc. cit.*, pp. 3, 17.

Two specimens from the Funafuti lagoon.

Garrett cites this from Fiji, Tonga, Samoa, Gilberts, Carolines, Cook's, Society, and Paumotus Islands.

MITRA ACUMINATA, *Swainson.*

Tryon, *loc. cit.*, p. 153, pl. xlv., fig. 312 ; Garrett, *loc. cit.*, pp. 5, 32.

Three examples from the Funafuti lagoon.

Garrett has recorded this from Fiji, Tonga, Samoa, Gilberts, Carolines, Cook's, Society, Paumotus, and Hawaiian Archipelagoes.

MITRA BRUNNEA, *Pease.*

Tryon, *loc. cit.*, p. 153, pl. xlv., fig. 301; Garrett, *loc. cit.*, pp. 5, 33.

A single specimen from Funafuti.

Garrett enumerates the known localities for this rather rare species : Fiji, Samoa, Carolines, Cook's, Society, Paumotus, and Hawaii. There is a specimen in this Museum from Howland's Island, North-Central Pacific ; and Langkavel reports it from the neighbouring Baker's Island. P. P. Carpenter asserts,[*] and Pease denies,[†] that *M. brunnea* is a synonym of *Strigatella fuscescens*, Pease, from Hawaii.

MITRA ASTRICTA, *Reeve.*

Tryon, *loc. cit.*, p. 154, pl. lxv., figs. 315, 318.

A single live specimen from the Funafuti lagoon.

Tryon quotes this from Hawaii.

MITRA LIMBIFERA, *Lamarck.*

Tryon, *loc. cit.*, p. 154, pl. xlv., figs. 322 – 326 ; Garrett, *loc. cit.*, pp. 5, 33.

Three specimens from Funafuti lagoon.

---

* Carpenter—Proc. Zool. Soc., 1865, p. 517.
† Pease—Am. Journ. Conch., iii., 1867, p. 233.

Garrett records this as *S. columbellæformis*, Kiener, from the Gilberts, Cook's, Society, and Paumotus.

MITRA LITTERATA, *Lamarck*.

Tryon, *loc. cit.*, p. 155, pl. xlvi., figs. 338, 339 ; Garrett, *loc. cit.*, pp. 5, 33.

In profusion in the rock pools on the ocean beach of Funafuti.

Garrett has traced this from Fiji, Tonga, Samoa, Gilberts, Carolines, Cook's, Society, and Paumotus, to Hawaii. Melvill and Standen note it from the Loyalties.* From Lord Howe Island, New Caledonia, and Fanning Island, there are instances in the Museum collection.

MITRA PAUPERCULA, *Linne*.

Tryon, *loc. cit.*, p. 156, pl. xlvi., fig. 340; Garrett, *loc. cit.*, pp. 5, 34.

Two specimens in company with the following species.

According to Garrett this form is confined to the West Pacific, ranging through Fiji, Tonga, Samoa, Gilberts, and Carolines. Melvill and Standen† recognise it from the Loyalty Islands.

MITRA VIRGATA, *Reeve*.

Tryon, *loc. cit.*, p. 156, pl. xlvi., fig. 341; Garrett, *loc. cit.*, pp. 5, 34.

Several specimens from the outer reef of Funafuti.

Garrett gives the range of this as identical with that of *M. paupercula.* It is in this Museum from New Caledonia.

TURRICULA GRUNERI, *Reeve*.

Tryon, *loc. cit.*, p. 168, pl. xlix., figs. 416, 418, 419; Garrett, *loc. cit.*, p. 47.

Two specimens were found on the lagoon beach at Funafuti.

Garrett reports this from Upolu, Samoa, and the Pelew Islands. It is represented in this Museum from New Caledonia, and the Gilberts.

TURRICULA ANGULOSA, *Kuster*.

Tryon, *loc. cit.*, p. 169, pl. l., figs. 431, 432 ; Garrett, *loc. cit.*, pp. 5, 37.

One specimen from Funafuti.

Found by Garrett in Fiji.

TURRICULA VARIATA, *Reeve*.

Tryon, *loc. cit.*, p. 193, pl. lvi., fig. 635 ; Garrett, *loc. cit.*, pp. 7, 61.

One specimen from Funafuti.

---

* Melvill & Standen—*Loc. cit.*, viii., p. 101.
† Melvill & Standen—*Loc. cit.*, viii.,ip. 101.

Taken by Garrett at Fiji, Samoa, Cook's, Society, and Paumotu Groups.

TURRICULA NODOSA, *Swainson.*

Tryon, *loc. cit.*, p. 193, pl. lvi., figs. 638–641 ; Garrett, *loc. cit.*, pp. 6, 53.

One dead specimen from Funafuti.

Garrett records this from Fiji, Tonga, Samoa, Gilberts, Carolines, Cook's, Society, Paumotus, and Hawaii. Melvill and Standen observe it from the Loyalties.* There is an example in this Museum from Niue.

TURRICULA PILSBRYI, sp. nov.

(Fig. 40).

Shell fusiform. Colour orange-buff, with a rosy apex. Whorls five, plus the protoconch. Sculpture—on the last whorl are six roundly swelling arcuate ribs, which arise at the suture and

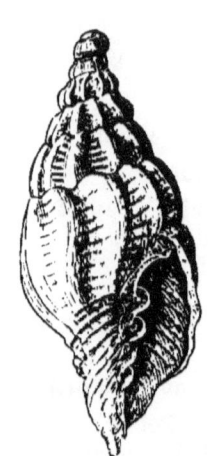

terminate at the basal constriction, but disappear on the final half whorl ; the antipenultimate has thirteen ribs. On ascending the spire, the ribs become comparatively more prominent, and on the earliest whorl are sharply constricted and angled at their upper third. On each whorl they alternate with those above and below. Between the ribs appear delicate and evenly-spaced, spiral grooves. Seven or eight broad, close, flat-topped lyræ are obliquely wound around the base. Protoconch two-whorled, globose, projecting on the right side, smooth ; anteriorly a spiral groove forecasts the constriction of a later whorl. In the unique specimen the lip is broken. The columella bears a tubercle at the posterior angle, it is then excavated ; the moderately straight pillar carries four, conspicuous, projecting plaits ; a callus is spread

Fig. 40.

over the preceding whorl. The throat is on its outer wall corrugated by a dozen raised spiral lines. Length 6, breadth 2½ mm.

Taken by the tangles hauled up on the outer western slope of the atoll, in eighty to forty fathoms, associated with *Gorgonidæ, Thetidos,* etc.

This species is a member of the subgenus *Pusia,* and seems well defined by the uniform colour, smooth, wave-like ribs, and basal constriction.

---

* Melvill & Standen—*Loc. cit.,* viii., p. 103.

Named in honour of the brilliant American Conchologist, who has so successfully laboured to place the systematic study of the Mollusca on a more scientific basis.

CYLINDRA DACTYLUS, *Linne.*

Tryon, *loc. cit.*, p. 197, pl. lvii., figs. 658, 664 ; Garrett, *loc. cit.*, pp. 7, 65.

Three specimens from the Funafuti lagoon.

Garrett found this at Fiji, Tonga, Samoa, Gilberts, Carolines, Society, Paumotus, and Hawaii. Melvill and Standen quote it from the Loyalties.* Examples from Woodlark Island (British New Guinea), and New Caledonia, are contained in this Museum.

ERATO SCHMELTZIANA, *Crosse.*

Tryon, Man. Conch. v., 1883, p. 11, pl. iv., figs. 54, 55.

A few specimens were collected on the beach of the Funafuti lagoon.

Previously reported only from Fiji.

MARGINELLA SANDWICENSIS, *Pease.*

Tryon, *loc. cit.*, p. 45, pl. xii., fig. 69.

Several dead shells were picked up on the beach of the Funafuti lagoon.

Tryon reports it from Hawaii and Fiji.

MARGINELLA IOTA, sp. nov.
(Fig. 41).

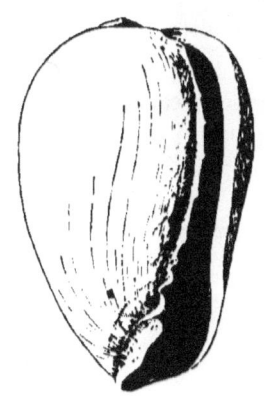

Shell ovate, truncate anteriorly, white, smooth. Spire slightly exserted. Aperture comparatively wide. Outer lip thick, sinuate, smooth within. Inner lip with three principal anterior plications and several remote subsidiary ones, deep within. Length 1·5, breadth ·95 mm.

Three specimens from the sand of the lagoon beach.

The only *Marginella* comparable in size, known from the tropical Pacific, is *M. mariei*, Crosse, whose broad shell and immersed spire easily distinguish it.

Fig. 41.

MARGINELLA PEASII, *Reeve.*

Tryon, *loc. cit.*, p. 53, pl. xiii., fig. 27.

Abundant in a dead state on the sandy beach of the lagoon.

* Melvill & Standen—*Loc. cit.*, viii., p. 103.

Hitherto only known from the Gilberts. *Volutella elongata (Marginella elliptica*, Redfield),* from Fanning Island, seems suspiciously close to this.

OLIVELLA SIMPLEX, *Pease.*

Tryon, *loc. cit.*, p. 72, pl. xvii., figs. 47, 48.

A single dead shell was found with the foregoing species.

Reported by its author from Upolu, Samoa, and Tongatabu, Tonga.

OLIVA GUTTATA, *Lamarck.*

Tryon, *loc. cit.*, p. 74, pl. xix., figs. 64 – 74.

A dead specimen was found on the beach of the lagoon.

In this Museum it is represented from Trinity Bay, North Queensland, New Caledonia, and New Hebrides.

OLIVA IRISANS, var. ERYTHROSTOMA, *Lamarck.*

Tryon, *loc. cit.*, p. 80, pl. i., fig. 3; pl. xxvi., figs. 53, 54; pl. xxvii., figs. 55–58; pl. xxxiv., fig. 53.

A few empty shells were found upon the beach.

Melvill and Standen mention this from Lifu. Specimens are included in the series of this Museum from Niuc, Tonga, and Erromanga (New Hebrides).

HARPA MINOR, *Lamarck.*

Tryon, *loc. cit.*, p. 99, pl. xli., figs. 69 – 72, 78.

Several dead shells were noticed on the lagoon beach.

Schmeltz records this from Fiji and the Gilberts, and Melvill and Standen from Lifu. It is in this Museum from the Solomons.

HARPA GRACILIS, *Broderip & Sowerby.*

Tryon, *loc. cit.*, p. 99, pl. xli., fig. 73.

A single dead shell of this rare species was taken on the lagoon beach.

H. Cuming discovered this at Anaa, Paumotus. Schmeltz gives it from the Gilberts and Rarotonga.

DRILLIA UNIZONALIS, *Lamarck.*

Tryon, Man. Conch., vi., 1884, p. 185, pl. ix., figs. 30, 33, 34, 38; pl. xxxii., fig. 48.

One specimen from Funafuti lagoon.

---

* Pease—Am. Journ. Conch., iii., 1867, p. 281, pl. xxiii., fig. 23.

Under the synonym of *D. vidua*, Reeve, this is quoted by Garrett* from Fiji and Wallis Island; by Melvill and Standen† from Lifu; and by Weinkauff‡ from Upolu, Samoa. I have collected it at Port Moresby, British New Guinea.

GLYPHOSTOMA PURPURASCENS, *Dunker*.

Dunker, Malak. Blatt., xviii., 1871, p. 160.

Clathurella pulchella, Garrett, Proc. Acad. Nat. Sci. Phil., 1873, p. 219, pl. iii., fig. 32.

Glyphostoma goubini, Hervier, Journ. de Conch., xliii., 1895(1896), p. 149; xliv., 1896 (1897), p. 75, pl. ii., fig. 17.

Seven specimens from the lagoon at Funafuti.

Tryon writes that *G. purpurascens* "is admitted by Mr. Garrett to be identical with his *C. pulchella*, over which it has two years' priority of publication."§ The figure and description of Father Hervier so exactly correspond to the others quoted, that I fear no contradiction in reducing his name to synonomy. Possibly the unfigured *C. rubicunda*, Gould,|| is the same species.

Dunker described it from Upolu (Samoa), Garrett from Fiji, and Hervier from Lifu (Loyalties). If the prior *Clathurella rubicunda*, Gould, is identical, the range includes the Loo Choo Islands.

GLYPHOSTOMA ALICEÆ, *Melvill & Standen*.

Melvill & Standen, Journ. Conch., viii., 1895, p. 95, pl. ii., fig. 15 (bad).

Three specimens from Funafuti agree generally with an authentic example from Lifu. The photographic illustration quoted is too indistinct to show details.

GLYPHOSTOMA ALICEÆ, *M. & S.*, var. TENERA, var nov.

This variety differs in sculpture from the preceding, having on the last whorl fifteen delicate costæ, where the typical form bears eight, thick and prominent ribs. At the anterior termination of these ribs, the variety has a more decided angle, followed by a more hollow base, than the species in chief.

Five specimens from the lagoon beach.

GLYPHOSTOMA MALLETI, *Recluz*.

Recluz, Journ. de Conch., iii., 1852, pl. x., fig. 2; Tryon, *loc. cit.*, p. 297, pl. xx., figs. 96, 100.

---

* Garrett—Proc. Acad. Nat. Sci. Phil., 1873, p. 218.
† Melvill & Standen—*Loc. cit.*, viii., p. 94.
‡ Weinkauff—Conch. Cab. (ii.), iv., 1, 1887, p. 60.
§ Tryon—*Loc. cit.*, p. 298.
|| Gould—Proc. Boston Soc. Nat. Hist., vii., 1861, p. 338.

A single specimen was taken in company with the *Gorgonidæ* described *ante* p. 308 – 320, by tangles hauled from eighty to forty fathoms on the outer and western slope of Funafuti. It differs considerably from a specimen (apparently typical) received from New Caledonia, being of a chrome-orange colour, with a pale peripheral band, 5 mm. long by 2 broad. Whereas the New Caledonian example is of a peach-blossom pink colour, 6¼ mm. long, 3 mm. broad, and of a stouter build. Both show the granulations noted in the original description which Dall points out as characteristic of the genus.*

Garrett found this in Samoa and Fiji, and Melvill and Standen received it in abundance from Lifu, Loyalties.†

THETIDOS, gen. nov.

A member of the Mangiliinæ, distinguished by three stout tubercles seated on the lip within the aperture, and by a globose, tilted, two-whorled protoconch, which is closely spirally grooved throughout.

The new species, which typifies this proposed new genus, stands apart from almost all Pleurotomidæ, with regard to the few large denticules which defend the aperture. The thickened lip and anal notch throw it into Tryon's subfamily Mangiliinæ, and among the members of that, *Glyphostoma* makes the nearest approach. *Glyphostoma* has smaller and more numerous denticules, and an apex which in *G. gabbii* is thus described by Dall :—" nucleus acute, three-whorled, the first whorl smooth, rounded, tilted, minute ; the others smooth, polished, keeled on the periphery."‡ This description fits others I have examined such as *G. malleti*. In various instances the protoconch of *Mangelia* is shown by Watson to have delicate, longitudinal ribbing. The genus *Clathurella* has a peculiar raised mesh-work over all the whorls of the protoconch, as here illustrated in the case of *C. irretita*, and which has been beautifully figured in several instances by Watson in the " Challenger " Report. The apex which Cossman gives as characteristic of *Clathurella* is, however, quite different.§

Opinions on the systematic importance of the Pleurotomoid protoconch are conflicting. Watson remarks that :—" sculpture and form of apex may probably serve as the safest basis of classification in the whole group."‖ On the contrary Dall has expressed his opinion that :—" so far as our knowledge goes, nuclear

* Dall—Bull. Mus. Comp. Zool., xviii., 1889, p. 108.
† Melvill & Standen—*Loc. cit.*, p. 402.
‡ Dall—*Loc. cit.*, p. 109.
§ Cossman—Essais de Palèoconchologie comparée, ii., 1896, p. 122.
‖ Watson—Chall. Rep. Zool., xv., 1886, p. 361.

characters have little absolute systematic value in this group, and their relative value remains to be determined."*

Even should little weight attach to the nuclear distinction of *Thetidos*, the aperture, so curiously imitating Sistrum or Pupa, may separate it from its kindred, only excepting *Clathurella idiomorpha*, Hervier,† and *Clathurella rugosa*, Mighels.‡ As those authors paid no special attention to the protoconch, I am unable to decide whether they should also enter my genus.

I have no information relative to the presence or absence of the operculum, since to obtain such would entail the destruction of the only shell. It may be that in this family the thickening of the lip, followed by the development of the labial teeth, and consequent narrowing of the aperture has accompanied the degeneration of the operculum. The safety of the animal being thus secured by the exchange of one defence for another.

THETIDOS MORSURA, sp. nov.

(Fig. 42).

Fig. 42.

Shell stout and strongly built, briefly conical, a little turreted, anteriorly narrowed suddenly with a short straight and truncate canal. Whorls five, exclusive of the protoconch. Colour dead white, except the two uppermost whorls and the protoconch, which are pale fawn. Sculpture—the last whorl has ten thick and prominent ribs, round at their base and summit, their own width apart, shouldered posteriorly and abruptly terminating anteriorly at the basal constriction. On each succeeding whorl the ribs alternate with those beneath. The revolving sculpture consists, on the last whorl, of eight, strong, elevated, equidistant, narrow spiral cords which over-ride the ribs, and five such which encircle the base, where vestigial ribs tend to dissect them into nodules ; on the penultimate whorl there are four to five cords visible. Protoconch tilted, two-whorled, and spirally grooved. Aperture narrow ; columella

---

* Dall—*Loc. cit.*, p. 75.

† Hervier—Journ. de Conch., xliv., 1896 (1897), p. 147 ; xlv., 1897, p. 110, pl. iii., fig. 3.

‡ Langkavel—Donum Bismarckianum, 1871, p. 2, pl. i., fig. 5.

excavate above, anteriorly ridged by the entrance of three of the basal cords which ascend obliquely; canal open, broad, short, truncated; outer lip much thickened externally by a heavy varix which is crossed and denticulated by the spiral sculpture; within the varix, and at right angles to it, the aperture proper has a second raised lip, and within that again are three large, equidistant tubercles, the largest and most prominent of which is that next the sinus; the anal sinus is moderately deep, scarcely mounts on the preceding whorl, and spreads a callus across two ribs. Length 5½, breadth 2½ mm.

One example, procured in eighty to forty fathoms by the tangles, with the preceding species.

MANGILIA HIMERTA, *Melvill & Standen.*

Melvill & Standen, Journ. Conch., viii., 1896, p. 281, pl. ix., fig. 17.

One example from the lagoon beach. Only before recorded from Lifu.

CLATHURELLA LACTEA, *Reeve.*

Reeve, Conch. Icon. i., 1843, Pleurotoma, pl. xv., sp. 123.

One specimen from the lagoon beach answers well to Reeve's illustration.

CLATHURELLA CLANDESTINA, *Deshayes.*

Tryon, *loc. cit.*, p. 298, pl. xix., fig. 67; pl. xx., fig. 81.

One specimen from the Funafuti lagoon, slighter and paler than the typical form. It is only 4 mm. long, and has a buff tip and two obscure buff bands on the back of the last whorl.

Pease found this in the Paumotus, Garrett in Fiji, and Hadfield at Lifu.* I collected a large form, 7 mm. in length, at Milne Bay, British New Guinea. According to the descriptions, *C. pumila*, Mighels, seems scarcely separable.

CLATHURELLA APICALIS, *Montrouzier.*

Montrouzier, Journ. de Conch., ix., 1861, p. 277, pl. xi., fig. 1.

Two worn specimens from the beach of the Funafuti lagoon.

Tryon† relegates this to the synonymy of *C. felina*, Hinds. As Reeve's miserable figure of this permits no comparison, I accept without criticism Hervier's assurance‡ that it is distinct.

* Melvill & Standen—*Loc. cit.*, viii., p. 402.
† Tryon—*Loc. cit.*, p. 293.
‡ Hervier—*Loc. cit.*, xlv., 1897, p. 101.

CLATHURELLA IRRETITA, sp. nov.

(Fig. 43).

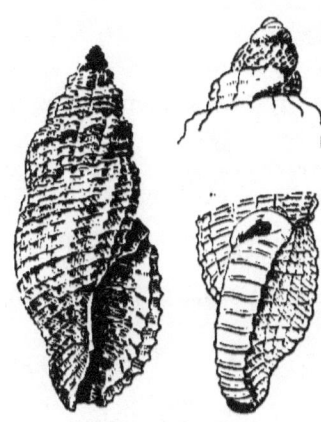

Shell ovate-fusiform, narrow, turretted and sharply angled below a sloping shoulder. Colour white, from the suture to the angle opaque, below the angle hyaline with opaque beads; protoconch buff yellow, a splash of the same on the anterior dorsal portion of the last whorl; a pale yellow thread, confined to one spiral cord, ascends each whorl below the angle, and another surrounds the last whorl below the periphery. Adult whorls four and a half. Sculpture—the last whorl bears fifteen longitudinal costæ which cross the flattened part of the whorl obliquely, here they are separated by twice their breadth; above the angle they bend and enlarge suddenly, towards the base they curve in and vanish at the basal constriction. On the penultimate whorl these costæ alternate with those below the suture. These longitudinal costæ are over-ridden by a series of fine sharp spiral cords knotted at each costa; the last whorl carrying four larger and more undulating ones above the angle and ten below it; on the base are six simple cords. Protoconch horny, mamillate, three and a half whorled, the larger sculptured with a raised network, contrasting sharply by colour and texture with the adult shell, which suddenly commences with a thick raised white tongue at the suture. Aperture narrow and elliptical, columella arched, overlaid by a callus which ends abruptly where the mouth narrows. Canal short and wide. Outer lip massive, ridged externally by a dozen transverse cords which denticulate the edges; within are seven weak entering ridges. The aperture mounts the preceding whorl to the height of two spiral cords, and encloses a deep wide anal notch with a prominent callus. Length 5, breadth 2 mm.

Fig. 43.

One specimen from the lagoon beach of Funafuti.

Closely allied to *Clathurella euzonata*, Hervier,* from which it differs by being narrower, sharper angled, and sculptured by finer and more numerous cords. With his species Hervier associates *C. bilineata*, Angas, and *C. bifasciatum*, Pease.

DAPHNELLA DELICATA, *Reeve.*

Reeve, Conch. Icon., i., 1846, "Pleurotoma," pl. xxxiv., sp. 310; Tryon, *loc. cit.*, p. 301, pl. xxvi., fig. 80.

---

* Hervier—Journ. de Conch., xliv., 1896 (1897), p. 143; *ibid.*, xlv., 1897, p. 102, pl. ii., fig. 6.

One specimen from the Funafuti lagoon beach.

It has been taken by Cuming at Marutea, Paumotus, and by Garrett at Tahiti.

DAPHNELLA LYMNEIFORMIS, *Kiener*.

Kiener, Coquilles Vivantes, Canaliferes, i., (n.d.), Pleurotome, p. 62, pl. xxii., fig. 3.

Two specimens from Funafuti appear to be the first recorded from the Central Pacific of this widely distributed form.

DAPHNELLA PUPOIDEA, *H. Adams*.

H. Adams, Proc. Zool. Soc., 1872, p. 14, pl. iii., fig. 27 ; Tryon, *loc. cit.*, p. 314, pl. xxxiv., fig. 92.

Mangilia victor, Sowerby, Proc. Malac. Soc., i., 1894, p. 45, pl. iv., fig. 19.

The single specimen from Funafuti is smaller and slighter than Adams' type specimen, from the New Hebrides, now in the Australian Museum. Melvill and Standen report it* from Lifu, Loyalties, and I have obtained it at Port Moresby, British New Guinea, and at Panie, New Caledonia. *Drillia pygmœa*, Dunker, seems to be suspiciously like this species.

DAPHNELLA THIASOTES, *Melvill & Standen*.

Mangilia thiasotes, Melvill & Standen, Journ. Conch., viii., 1896, p. 284, pl. ix., fig. 21.

A more complete account than is usually given by these authors enables me to satisfactorily identify a single specimen from Funafuti with their species from Lifu. They confess, " We know of no pleurotomoid shell which presents the same characteristics." If specific characters were thus alluded to in a shell described as new, the remark would be superfluous, and I therefore presume that generic characters are intended. It is obvious that this species is a close ally of such a shell as Angas described as *Purpura anomala*. Prof. R. Tate first pointed out that this latter was one of the Pleurotomidæ, allied to *M. vincenti*, Crosse.† In consonance with Tryon's classification, it is therefore here termed *Daphnella thiasotes*.

CONUS LITERATUS, *Linne*.

Tryon, *loc. cit.*, p. 10, pl. ii., figs. 17 – 19 ; Garrett, Journ. Conch., i., 1878, pp. 354, 360.

I purchased a specimen of this from a native at Nukulailai.

---

* Melvill & Standen—*Loc. cit.*, viii., p. 94.
† Tate—Proc. Linn. Soc. N.S.W., v., 1881, p. 131.

H. Cuming collected a form of this at Tahiti and Anaa, Paumotus.* Garrett found it in Fiji, the Gilberts, the Carolines, and Society Islands. In an excellent "Catalogue of the Cones of New Caledonia," by Crosse and Marie,† this is recorded from the mainland, Ile Art, and the Loyalty Group. In this Museum it is also represented from British New Guinea, Erromanga (New Hebrides), and the Bampton Reef (Coral Sea). Throughout the Pacific, this shell is greatly esteemed as material for native ornaments.

CONUS TESSELLATUS, *Born.*

Tryon, *loc. cit.*, p. 11, pl. ii., figs. 26, 27 ; Garrett, *loc. cit.*, pp. 355, 365.

A couple of specimens were procured at Funafuti.

Garrett reports this from Fiji, Samoa, Gilberts, Carolines, Cook's, Society, and Hawaii. Crosse and Marie mention this from Balade and Ile Art, New Caledonia. In this Museum are specimens from the New Hebrides and Torres Straits.

CONUS PULICARIUS, *Hwass.*

Tryon, *loc. cit.*, p. 19, pl. iv., fig. 68 ; pl. v., fig. 69 ; Garrett, *loc. cit.*, pp. 355, 362.

Two examples were obtained at Funafuti.

Garrett records this from Fiji, Tonga, Samoa, Gilberts, Carolines, Cook's, Society, Paumotus, and Marquesas Islands. Cuming observed this at Tahiti‡ ; Crosse and Marie at Ile Art and New Caledonia ; and Melvill and Standen at Lifu. Tryon mentions it from New Guinea, and specimens are in this Museum from Queensland, the Solomons, and the Gilberts.

CONUS HEBRAEUS, *Linne.*

Tryon, *loc. cit.*, p. 20, pl. v., figs. 75, 77; pl. xxvii., fig. 13; Garrett, *loc. cit.*, pp. 354, 360.

Abundant on the outer reef in rock pools at Funafuti, and I noted it also at Nukulailai.

Garrett cites this from Fiji, Tonga, Samoa, Gilberts, Carolines, Cook's, Society, Paumotus, and Hawaii. Crosse and Marie quote it from New Caledonia. In this Museum it is shown from the Louisiades, Erromanga, New Hebrides, and Lord Howe Island.

The native name on Funafuti is "miri." At Port Moresby the natives call it "ahukura."

---

* Reeve—Conch. Icon., i., Conus, 1843, pl. xxxii., sp. 178.
† Crosse & Marie—Journ. de Conch., 1874, p. 344.
‡ Reeve—*Loc. cit.*, pl. xvii., sp. 94.

CONUS HEBRAEUS, var. VERMICULATUS, *Hwass.*

A few of this colour variety occurred as usual with the typical form.

CONUS CEYLONENSIS, *Hwass.*

Tryon, *loc. cit.*, p. 23, pl. vi., figs. 94 – 100.

Abundant in the rock pools of the outer reef of Funafuti, in association with the preceding species. Numerous colour varieties are represented, among which is the var. *sponsalis*, Chemnitz.

Cuming collected this at Marutea, Paumotus* ; Crosse and Marie report it from Ile Art, New Caledonia ; and Melvill and Standen from Lifu. In a catalogue of the shells of Fitzroy Island,† Brazier notes it from there and from San Christoval, Solomons.

CONUS VEXILLUM, *Gmelin.*

Tryon, *loc. cit.*, p. 39, pl. xi., figs. 12*a*, 13, 14 ; Garrett, *loc. cit.*, pp. 356, 365.

One imperfect shell was purchased from a native at Funafuti.

Garrett found this in the Fiji, Tonga, Samoa, Gilberts, Cook's, Paumotus, and Hawaii Groups. Crosse and Marie mention this from New Caledonia, Ile Art, and Lifu ; Tryon from Samoa ; and there is a specimen in this Museum from Torres Straits. I have also collected it at Ballina, N.S. Wales.

CONUS RATTUS, *Hwass.*

Tryon, *loc. cit.*, p. 41, pl. xii., figs. 25, 27.

A single living specimen was taken under a stone in the Funafuti lagoon.

Cuming saw this at Tahiti, and Anaa, Paumotus‡ ; Crosse and Marie record it from Lifu and New Caledonia, and Weinkauff from Tonga.§ A specimen from the Bampton Reef, Coral Sea, is in this Museum.

CONUS CAPITANEUS, *Linne.*

Tryon, *loc. cit.*, p. 40, pl. xii., figs. 21 – 24 ; pl. xi., figs. 17, 18. Garrett, *loc. cit.*, pp. 354, 358.

One dead and immature shell from Funafuti.

Garrett found this in Fiji, Tonga, Samoa, Gilberts and Carolines. Crosse and Marie mention this from Ile Art, New Caledonia, and Brazier from Fitzroy Island, Queensland ; Torres Straits ; Hall Sound, British New Guinea ; Fiji, New Ireland, New Britain

---

* Reeve—*Loc. cit.*, pl. xx., sp. 100.
† Brazier—Journ. Conch., ii., 1870, p. 190.
‡ Reeve—*Loc. cit.*, pl. xv., sp. 78.
§ Weinkauff—Conch. Cab., 1873, Conus, p. 134.

and the Solomons. A specimen from the Bampton Reef is in this Museum.

CONUS LIVIDUS, *Hwass.*

Tryon, *loc. cit.*, p. 45, pl. xiii., figs. 54 – 57 ; Garrett, *loc. cit.*, pp. 354, 360.

One specimen was found alive under a stone in the Funafuti lagoon.

Garrett saw this in Fiji, Tonga, Samoa, Gilberts, Carolines, Cook's, Society, Paumotus, Marquesas and Hawaii. By Cuming it was taken in the Society Islands ; Melvill and Standen have it from the Loyalty. Specimens in this Museum extend the range to Woodlark Island, British New Guinea and the Solomons.

CONUS LIVIDUS, var. FLAVIDUS, *Lamarck.*

Tryon, *loc. cit.*, p. 44, pl. xiii., figs. 48 - 50.

Abundant alive under stones in the Funafuti lagoon.

Cuming collected this at Tahiti, Crosse and Marie cite it from Ile Art, New Caledonia ; Smith from the Solomons, Fiji, and Tonga* ; and Brazier from Torres Straits and Hall Sound, British New Guinea.† An Hawaiian specimen is contained in this Museum.

CONUS VITULINUS, *Hwass.*

Tryon, *loc. cit.*, p. 51, pl. xiv., figs. 86, 87 ; pl. xv., fig. 88.

One dead specimen from Funafuti.

Crosse and Marie cite this from the Loyalty Islands, Ile Art and Balade, New Caledonia. Brazier found it at Fitzroy Island, Queensland, Torres Straits, New Britain and New Ireland.

CONUS CATUS, *Hwass.*

Tryon, *loc. cit.*, p. 63, pl. xx., figs. 6 – 10 ; Garrett, *loc. cit.*, pp. 354, 358.

A single worn specimen from Funafuti.

Cuming collected this at Tahiti ; Crosse and Marie record it from New Caledonia and the Loyalty Group. This Museum has a specimen from Hawaii. Garrett found it in Fiji, Tonga, Samoa, Gilberts, Carolines, Cook's, Society, Paumotus and Hawaii.

CONUS NUSSATELLA, *Linne.*

Tryon, *loc. cit.*, p. 80, pl. xxv., fig. 35 ; Garrett, *loc. cit.*, pp. 355, 362.

Mr. G. Sweet obtained one specimen.

Garrett notes this from Fiji, Tonga, Samoa, Gilberts, Carolines, Cook's, Society, Paumotus and Hawaii.

---

* Smith—Proc. Zool. Soc., 1891, p. 400.
† Brazier—Proc. Linn. Soc. N.S.W., i., 1877, p. 288.

Conus striatus, *Linne.*

Tryon, *loc. cit.*, p. 85, pl. xxvi., fig. 67 ; Garrett, *loc. cit.*, pp. 355, 364.

A single empty shell from Funafuti.

Garrett collected this at Fiji, Tonga, Samoa, Gilberts, Carolines, Cook's, Society, and Hawaii. Crosse and Marie record this from the east coast of New Caledonia, and the Islands of Art and Lifu. Brazier has noted it from Fitzroy Island, Queensland, Torres Straits, New Ireland and New Britain ; and Smith from the Solomons. In this Museum are specimens from Erromanga, New Hebrides, and the Bampton Reef, Coral Sea.

Conus geographus, *Linne.*

Tryon, *loc. cit.*, p. 88, pl. xxviii, fig. 84; pl. xxix., fig. 85 ; Garrett, *loc. cit.*, pp. 354, 360.

A native of Funafuti presented me with a fine specimen, 120 mm. in length.

Garrett saw this at Fiji, Samoa, Gilberts, Carolines, Society and Paumotus. Crosse and Marie mention this from the Islands of Loyalty, Art and Pines, New Caledonia. This Museum possesses representatives from Fiji, the Solomon Islands and Erromanga, New Hebrides.

Conus tulipa, *Linne.*

Tryon, *loc. cit.*, p. 87, pl. xxviii., figs. 80, 81 ; Garrett, *loc. cit.*, pp. 355, 365.

I picked up a single specimen on the western beach of Funafuti.

Garrett obtained this at Fiji, Tonga, Samoa, Gilberts, Cook's, Society, Paumotus, Marquesas and Hawaii. Crosse and Marie note it from the Islands of Lifu, Art and Pines, New Caledonia. Examples from Torres Straits and Erromanga, New Hebrides, exist in this Museum.

Conus auratus, *Lamarck.*

Tryon, *loc. cit.*, p. 93, pl. xxxi., fig. 30 ; Garrett, *loc. cit.*, pp. 354, 357.

One dead shell from the lagoon beach of Funafuti.

Found by Cuming at Anaa, Paumotus, and noted by Crosse and Fischer from the Loyalty. In this Museum are instances from the Gilberts and Erromanga, New Hebrides. Garrett collected this at Fiji, Gilberts and Paumotus.

Terebra crenulata, *Linne.*

Tryon, Man. Conch., vii., 1885, p. 8, pl. i., figs. 1, 2, 6.

Several imperfect specimens were observed on the lagoon beach of Funafuti.

Hinds remarks this from the Society and Marquesas, and Melvill and Standen from Lifu; this Museum contains it from Pipon Island and New Caledonia.

TEREBRA DIMIDIATA, *Linne.*

Tryon, *loc. cit.*, p. 9, pl. i., figs. 4, 13.

Fragments only of this were collected at Funafuti by myself, but Mr. G. Sweet showed me a whole one.

Hinds reports this from Tahiti; Melvill and Standen from Lifu. It is in this Museum from British New Guinea, and Erromanga and Aneiteum, New Hebrides.

TEREBRA MACULATA, *Linne.*

Tryon, *loc. cit.*, p. 9, pl. i., figs 9, 10.

This shell is a rarity on Funafuti, and I was unable to personally obtain a specimen, though I identified the species from one purchased from the natives by another member of our party. A specimen was also obtained by Mr. G. Sweet. It was formerly of great value to the inhabitants of this and other Pacific Islands, who employed it as a cutting or boring edge for certain tools.* Dr. Hinds, who found a dwarf form at Hao Atoll, Paumotus, remarks :—" In the Pacific, the animal is eaten as food, and the shell, ground at an angle, was much in use as a chisel in the construction of the canoes."†

The "Chevert" Expedition obtained this in Torres Straits. Melvill and Standen note it from Lifu. I collected it at Port Moresby, British New Guinea, where the natives knew it as " bodoa."

TEREBRA SUBULATA, *Linne.*

Tryon, *loc. cit.*, p. 10, pl. i., fig. 3; pl. iii., fig. 35.

One specimen was found by Mr. G. Sweet.

Hinds found it at Hao and Tahiti. It is represented from the Solomons, New Caledonia, and Hawaii in this Museum.

TEREBRA TIGRINA, *Gmelin.*

Tryon, *loc. cit.*, p. 10, pl. i., fig. 11.

Mr. G. Sweet obtained two examples. Reported by Tryon from Hawaii, and represented in this Museum from the New Hebrides.

TEREBRA AFFINIS, *Gray.*

Tryon, *loc. cit.*, p. 14 pl. ii., figs. 18, 22.

Two worn shells were taken on the Funafuti beach.

---

* See *ante* pp. 249, 259.
† R. B. Hinds—Thes. Conch., i., 1847, p. 150.

Gᴏ

Tryon quotes this from Fiji, and Melvill and Standen from Lifu. Schmeltz mentions it from Tahiti and Upolu, Samoa.* Specimens from the New Hebrides are in the possession of this Museum.

SOLIDULA SULCATA, *Gmelin.*

Pilsbry, Man. Conch., xv., 1893, p. 143, pl. xx*a*, figs. 39, 46, 47, 48.

Several specimens from the lagoon beach.

This abundant, variable and widespread species has been reported from Queensland and New Caledonia by Brazier, and from Tahiti by Pilsbry. It is represented in the Museum Collection from Guam in the Ladrones and from Aneiteum in the New Hebrides.

TORNATINA VOLUTA, *Quoy & Gaimard.*

Pilsbry, Man. Conch., xv., 1893, p. 195, pl. xxii., figs. 29, 30, 31.

Abundant on the lagoon beach.

Taken originally at Guam in the Ladrones by the "Astrolabe," it was afterwards found in Torres Straits by the "Chevert" and in Fiji by the "Challenger." Melvill and Standen note it from the Loyalty Islands, and I have myself collected it at Noumea, New Caledonia.

TORNATINA HADFIELDI, *Melvill & Standen.*

Melvill & Standen, Journ. Conch., viii., 1896, p. 314 ; pl. xi., fig. 80.

Some broken specimens from the lagoon beach appear to belong to this species, which Melvill and Standen describe from Lifu, and which I have also taken at Panie, New Caledonia.

RETUSA WAUGHIANA, sp. nov.
(Fig. 44).

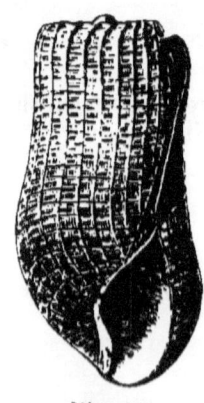

Shell subcylindrical, swollen below, sharply truncated above, produced and rounded anteriorly. Colour porcelain white, glossy. Sculpture—longitudinal, irregularly spaced ribs traverse the whole shell, anteriorly they are weak threads, posteriorly they wax stouter and form tubercles as they obliquely mount the vertex. Between these the shell is closely girt by about forty spiral grooves and their complementary ridges. Whorls four, the earlier ascending, the last descending. Suture deeply channelled. Apex mamillate, rising above the crown. Aperture very oblique, racquet shaped. Outer lip springing from the wall considerably below the vertex, rounded posteriorly, parallel with the body whorl as far

Fig. 44.

---

* Schmeltz—Mus. Godeffroy Cat. v., 1874, p. 134.

as the waist of the shell, then curving outwards. Columella broad, sinuate, folded over a slight umbilical chink. Callus on body whorl distinct, forming a decided angle posteriorly. Length 1¾, breadth 1 mm.

Three specimens from the lagoon beach.

This species perhaps stands nearest to *R. amphizosta*, Watson,[*] from which it is easily distinguished by the even more pulled anterior half, the descent of the last whorl, and by the coarser, more prominent sculpture. The young shells differ altogether in contour from the adult, but may be recognised by their peculiar sculpture.

This novelty is named in honour of my accomplished friend, Lieutenant A. Waugh, R.N., of H.M.S. "Penguin," who, during the Expedition to Funafuti, as on many previous occasions, afforded his hearty aid and sympathy to every scientific undertaking.

ATYS CYLINDRICA, *Helbling.*

Pilsbry, Man. Conch., xv., 1893, p. 265, pl. xxxiii., figs. 60–64.

Abundant on the lagoon beach.

This common Pacific shell ranges in Australia from Torres Straits southwards to Port Stephens, N.S.W.; the "Challenger" met it in Fiji; I took it at Noumea, New Caledonia, and the Museum has received from Mr. N. Hardy a specimen he collected at Aneiteum, New Hebrides.

ATYS HYALINA, *Watson.*

Pilsbry, *loc. cit.*, p. 271, pl. xxxii., fig. 36.

A single broken specimen from the Funafuti lagoon agrees with specimens in the Museum from a type locality, Torres Straits. The "Challenger" procured this from Fiji, and doubtfully from Honolulu.

ATYS DENTIFERA, *A. Adams.*

Pilsbry, *loc. cit.*, p. 276, pl. xxvii., fig. 81.

The occurrence of several specimens on the lagoon beach of Funafuti points to a range across the whole Pacific, since this habitat is intermediate between Marutea, Paumotus, in the extreme east, where it was first discovered by Hugh Cuming, and Torres Straits in the extreme west, where it was taken by the "Challenger," as also at Fiji. Mr. H. Smithurst has presented to the Museum a specimen he collected at Milne Bay, British New Guinea.

---

[*] Watson—Chall. Rep., Zool., xv., 1886, p. 652, pl. xlviii., fig. 11.

ATYS DACTYLUS, sp. nov.

(Fig. 45).

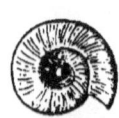

Shell date shaped, truncated above and below, minutely perforate above, deeply and narrowly umbilicate below. Colour white, glossy. Sculpture—from sixty to seventy, irregularly waved, narrow, shallow grooves girdle the shell, between which are smooth, flat topped lyræ, two or three times their breadth; these are crossed at irregular intervals by fine and coarse growth lines. The aperture is vertical, longer than the shell, narrowly arched, dilated above and below, rather effuse anteriorly. Above, the lip rises from the centre of the apical crater and folding back almost covers the perforation; the outer lip is straight and simple; the columella broadly reflexed, emarginate without, tuberculate within, a short tongue of callus extends a little distance upwards along the body whorl. Length $4\frac{1}{2}$, breadth $2\frac{1}{2}$ mm.

Fig. 45.

One specimen from the lagoon beach.

This species appears to approach nearest to *A. jeffreysi*, Weinkauff, from the Mediterranean, which served Monterosato as type for his genus *Roxaniella*.

CYLICHNA ERECTA, sp. nov.

(Fig. 46).

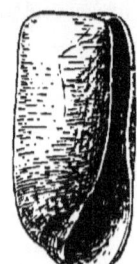

Shell cylindrical, truncated above, bevelled outwardly round the vertex, rounded below and compressed around the basal axis. Colour white. Sculpture—the only specimen is too worn for exact description; it seems to have been girt by numerous broad and shallow spiral grooves. Aperture nearly perpendicular; lip produced medially; columella broadly reflected, apparently minutely plicated. Spire umbilicate, a shallow crater into which each whorl descends by steps. Length 4, breadth $1\frac{3}{4}$ mm.

A single rather worn example from the lagoon beach.

Fig. 46.

This species appears to be quite distinct from others of the genus. Those that share the cylindrical shape being *C. discus*, Watson, more truncated anteriorly; *C. protracta*, Gould, three times larger; *C. involuta*, Adams, *C. cylindracea*, Pennant, and *C. alba*, Brown, which appear to have the spire covered. No comparison can be instituted with a mass of unfigured species with which authors (Adams being chief sinner) have oppressed descriptive conchology.

HAMINEA VITREA, *A. Adams.*

Pilsbry, *loc. cit.*, p. 370, pl. xl., fig. 83.

Two specimens from the lagoon beach.

The "Chevert" Expedition took this species in Torres Straits. It occurred to me at Panie, New Caledonia; and under the synonym of *H. tenera*, A. Adams, Melvill and Standen record it from the Loyalties.

CYLINDROBULLA SCULPTA, *Nevill.*

Pilsbry, *loc. cit.*, p. 381, pl. xlii., figs. 36 – 38.

Two living specimens from shallow water in the lagoon, correspond fairly to the above quotation. This Cingalese species has not been noticed before in the Pacific.

AKERA APERTA, sp. nov.
(Fig. 47).

Shell small, fragile, transparent, oval. Whorls two and a half, last sloping on the shoulder, then subangled and rounded below; sculptured by close, regular growth lines. Apex truncate. Spire minute, visible through a flat, glossy plate, which continues into a rib bordering the sutural notch. Aperture as long as the shell, much dilated and effuse below, narrowed above to the broad and deep sinus; outer lip arched forward above the middle; columella very concave with a narrow sharply reflexed edge. Length 5, breadth 4 mm.

Three specimens from sand on the lagoon beach.

This curious shell agrees with *Akera* in having the spire at the vertex and in the open aperture, but it approaches *Cylindrobulla* in the more involute spire. I am not satisfied that this may not be the young of the preceding species, but as no information is published on the immature stages of these genera, it seemed well to describe my material, even at the risk of increasing synonomy.

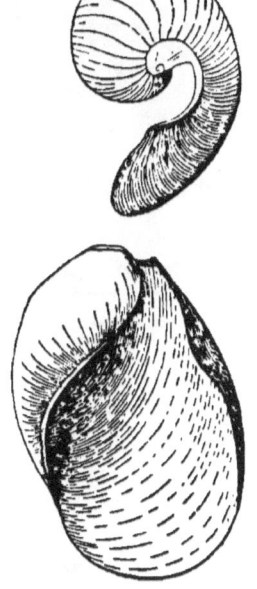

Fig. 47.

HYDATINA AMPLUSTRE, *Linne.*

Pilsbry, *loc. cit.*, p. 390, pl. xliv., figs. 1 – 6.

An immature specimen from the lagoon beach.

So conspicuous a shell is readily observed ; Pilsbry quotes Pacific records embracing most archipelagoes between Queensland and Hawaii.

HYDATINA PHYSIS, *Linne.*

Pilsbry, *loc. cit.*, p. 387, pl. xlv., figs. 14, 15, 16, 17.

Mr. G. Sweet found a young shell of this world wide species.

RINGICULA PARVULA, sp. nov.

(Fig. 48).

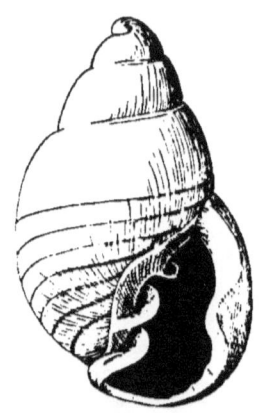

Fig. 48.

Shell very small, broad, solid, milk-white and glossy. Whorls rounded, chanelled at the suture ; incised by half a dozen sharp narrow grooves at and below the periphery. The mouth armature consists of a large blunt tooth in the middle of the outer lip, an elevated and much compressed one on the body whorl and two others, distant, rounded and oblique on the columella. Length 1·6, breadth 1 mm.

Differs in dentition and contour from *R. mariei,* Morelet, and *R. acuta* v. *minuta,* H. Adams, and in its minute size from all others of the genus.

One specimen from the lagoon beach.

ELYSIA NIGROPUNCTATA, *Pease,* var. SANGUINEA, var. nov.

(Fig. 49).

Fig. 49.

This variety differs from the type figured by Pease or Bergh* by being smaller by one third, and having the tentacles and mantle border coloured a vivid crimson.

One specimen was collected at low water on the extreme outer edge of the windward reef.

Perhaps *E. marginatus,* Pease, is but another colour variety of the same species.

PLECOTREMA BELLUM, *H. & A. Adams.*

Sykes, Proc. Malac. Soc., i., 1895, p. 242.

In reference to this species, Souverbie pathetically remarks that the wretched work of the Adams permits of no precise identification. Their baneful seed has here produced the usual crop of synonomy. My determination of a shell, once collected on

---

* Pease—Am. Journ. Conch., vi., 1871, p. 304, pl. xxii., fig. 2 *a, b, c, d.*; Bergh—Journ. Mus. Godeffroy, i., 1873, p. 80, pl. ix., fig. 7.

the lagoon beach of Funafuti, rests on a statement by Sykes that *P. bellum* equals *P. souverbiei*, Montrouzier, and upon the illustrations of that, which he omitted to quote.*

The range recorded in the Central Pacific is New Caledonia, Loyalty, Taviuni, Fiji, Paumotus, and Gambier.

PLECOTREMA MORDAX, *Dohrn.*

Langkavel, Donum Bismarckianum, 1871, p. 30, pl. iii., figs. 8 *a. b.*

Two specimens from the lagoon beach.

This species, known only from Tahiti and the Paumotus, is perhaps equivalent to the earlier but unfigured *P. striatum*, Philippi.

MELAMPUS FASCIATUS, *Deshayes.*

Kuster, Conch. Cab., 2nd ed., i., Auriculacea, 1844, p. 33, pl. v., figs. 9 – 11.

Of this species, Mr. G. Sweet obtained several shells.

The following records from the Central Pacific are quoted by Tapparone Canefri† : New Guinea, New Ireland, New Hebrides, New Caledonia, Fiji, Samoa, Society, and Ellice. Further instances from the Solomons, Queensland, Carolines, Marquesas, and Hawaii, are furnished by this Museum.

MELAMPUS LUTEUS, *Quoy & Gaimard.*

Kuster, *loc. cit.*, p. 29, pl. vi., figs. 1 – 3.

Extremely abundant at and above high water-mark, among stones and vegetation.

Tapparone Canefri traces this through the following archipelagoes : New Guinea, New Ireland, New Hebrides, New Caledonia, Samoa, Ellice, Gilberts, Society, and Carolines. Crosse‡ reports it from Woodlark Island on the authority of Montrouzier ; and Museum material enables me to add the Solomons.

TORNATELLINA OBLONGA, *Pease.*

Garrett, Proc. Zool. Soc., 1887, p. 187.

Several living specimens were collected at Funafuti under sticks and stones. Mousson did not record this from the Ellice. "Inhabits," says Garrett, "all the groups from the Marquesas and Paumotus to the Viti Islands."

TORNATELLINA CONICA, *Mousson.*

Garrett, *loc. cit.*, p. 187.

---

* Montrouzier—Journ. de Conch., x., 1862, pl. ix., fig. 12 ; Gassies—Faune Conch. de la Nouvelle Calèdonie, 1863, pl. vi., fig. 23.

† Tapparone Canefri—Ann. Mus. Gen., xix., 1883, p. 288.

‡ Crosse—Journ. de Conch., xlii., 1894, p. 323.

Though Græffe found this at Funafuti it escaped my observation. It has the same range as the preceding species, and inhabits the same station.

VERTIGO PEDICULUS, *Shuttleworth.*

Garrett, *loc. cit.*, p. 188.

This widespread species occurred to me at Funafuti as it also did to Græffe.

To the extensive synonymy compiled by Garrett I would suggest the addition of *P. palmyra*, Stol.* and *P. selebensis*, Tapp. Can.†

STENOGYRA GRACILIS, *Hutton.*

Hutton, Journ. Asiat. Soc. Bengal, iii., 1834, p. 93.

Under the synonym of *S. juncea*, Gould, this widespread species has already been recorded from Funafuti. Like Græffe I found it in abundance. A recently described Australian species, *S. interioris*, Tate,‡ seems to me to be synonymous.

ENDODONTA MODICELLA, *Ferussac.*

Pilsbry, Man. Conch. ix., 1894, p. 35.

This widely distributed species is common at Funafuti, where under the name of *E. vicaria*, it has already been recorded by Mousson. To the synonymy arranged by Pilsbry I would add, as the result of study of authentic specimens, *Charopa rotumana*, Smith.§

ENDODONTA DECEMPLICATA, *Mousson.*

Mousson, Journ. de Conch., xxi., 1873, p. 105.

This species was found by Græffe at Nukufetau and Vaitupu, but was not observed by me at Funafuti.

TROCHONANINA SAMOENSIS, *Mousson.*

Garrett, *loc. cit.*, p. 171 ; Mousson, *loc. cit.*, p. 104.

I found this common on Funafuti. Græffe took it on Niutao, Vaitupu, Nui, and Nukufetau. Garrett reports it as " common in the Tonga, Cook's, and Samoa Islands, and rare in the Marquesas."

---

* Stoliczka—Journ. Asiat. Soc. Bengal, xlii., p. 32, pl. iii., fig. 3 *a*, *b*.
† Tapperone Canefri—Ann. Mus. Gen. xx., 1883-4, p. 171, pl. i., figs. 12, 13.
‡ Tate—Horn Explor. Exped., Zool., p. 203, pl. xviii., fig. 14.
§ Smith—Ann. Mag. Nat. Hist. (vi.), xx., 1897, p. 520.

THE MOLLUSCA OF FUNAFUTI.

Part II.—Pelecypoda and Brachiopoda.

By CHARLES HEDLEY,

Conchologist, Australian Museum.

H∎

XVIII

THE MOLLUSCA.

Part II.—Pelecypoda and Brachiopoda.

By CHARLES HEDLEY,

Conchologist, Australian Museum.

ANOMIA, sp.

A few disassociated upper valves, not specifically recognisable, were gathered on the lagoon beach of Funafuti.

ARCA ZEBRA, *Swainson.*

Reeve, Conch. Icon., ii., 1844, Arca, pl. xi., sp. 69.

Abundant under stones at low water in the lagoon. In this Museum there are specimens from Trinity Bay, Queensland.

It is doubtful whether *A. occidentalis*, Philippi, is distinct. If not, the species has a circumequatorial range.

ARCA MACULATA *Sowerby.*

Reeve, *loc. cit.*, pl. xi., sp. 71.

One living specimen obtained in the lagoon.

First found by Cuming at Marutea, in the Paumotus. Specimens are in this Museum from Aneiteum, New Hebrides.

ARCA RETICULATA, *Gmelin.*

Reeve, *loc. cit.*, pl. xvi., spp. 108, 112 (as *A. divaricata*, Sowerby).

Several disassociated valves of this world-wide species were observed on the lagoon beach.

The synonymy and range of this species have been examined at length by Lischke.*

ARCA VELATA, *Sowerby.*

Reeve, *loc. cit.*, pl. xii., sp. 79.

Common in blocks of coral in shallow water in the lagoon.

First obtained at Marutea, Paumotus, by Cuming.

---

* Lischke—Japan Meeres conchylien, ii., 1871, p. 142, iii., 1874, p. 107. Smith adds *A. dubia*, Baird, to the list—Proc. Zool. Soc., 1891, p. 431. Further notes will be found in the Proc. Linn. Soc. N.S.W. (2), ix., 1894, p. 180; Trans. Roy. Soc. S.A., xix., 1895, p. 261; and Trans. Wagner Free Inst. Sci., iii., 1898, p. 628.

ARCA TENELLA, *Reeve*.

Reeve, *loc. cit.*, pl. xiv., sp. 91.

One living and one dead specimen were taken in the lagoon.

SEPTIFER EXCISUS, *Wiegmann*.

Reeve, Conch. Icon., x., 1857, Mytilus, pl. iv., sp. 13.

Separate valves were common on the lagoon beach. I once found it alive in a block of perforated dead coral. This species does not seem to have been reported from the Pacific.

MODIOLA AUSTRALIS, *Gray*.

Reeve, *loc. cit.*, Modiola, pl. v., sp. 21.

Attached to coral blocks in the lagoon.

The species I thus identify has a wide range. It occurs along the Australian coast south to Sydney. Museum examples show it from the Gilberts, Lifu, and New Caledonia.

LITHOPHAGA TERES, *Philippi*.

Reeve, *loc. cit.*, Lithodomus, pl. iii., sp. 13.

Abundant; boring coral with the following species.

Schmeltz records it from Rarotonga, and Smith from Bowen, Queensland. It is in this Museum from Port Molle and Port Curtis, Queensland; and New Caledonia.

LITHOPHAGA LEVIGATA, *Quoy & Gaimard*.

Quoy and Gaimard, Voy. "Astrolabe," Zool. iii., 1835, p. 464, pl. lxxviii., figs. 17, 18.

Abundant at low water level, boring in coral blocks in the lagoon.

This species has been omitted from the Monographs of Reeve and Dunker, and indeed from subsequent literature generally. From the account quoted above, I have little doubt that it is the species commonly known as *Lithodomus malaccanus*, Reeve. It is a usual companion of the previous species. Under Reeve's name, Schmeltz quotes it from Tahiti, and Smith from Torres Straits. It is in this Museum from New Caledonia, and Tupuselei, British New Guinea.

PLICATULA IMBRICATA, *Menke*.

Sowerby, Thesaurus Conch., i., 1847, p. 437, pl. xc., fig. 6, pl. xci., figs. 15–18.

A few small specimens found alive in shallow water in the lagoon, adhering to dead shells, are with doubt so identified.

SPONDYLUS OCELLATUS, *Reeve.*

Reeve, Conch. Icon., ix., Spondylus, 1856, pl. xii., sp. 43.

An odd and worn valve from the lagoon beach is referred to this species.

Melvill and Standen report it from Lifu.

LIMA BULLATA, *Sowerby.*

Sowerby, Thes. Conch., i., 1847, p. 84, pl. xx., figs. 32, 33.

A single valve of a young individual is ascribed to this species, which ranges along the east Australian coast to Tasmania.

LIMA TENERA, *Chemnitz.*

Sowerby, *loc. cit.*, p. 84, pl. xxi., figs. 2, 3, 10, 11, 13.

One valve, apparently the young of this species, was obtained by tangles at forty to eighty fathoms.

Pacific localities for this species, noted in the "Challenger" Report, are Fiji, and Sir C. Hardy Island, off North Queensland. Melvill and Standen mention it from Lifu.

LIMA SQUAMOSA, *Lamarck.*

Sowerby, *loc. cit.*, p. 84, pl. xxi., figs. 1, 18.

This world-wide species occurred alive in the lagoon.

LIMA ANGULATA, *Sowerby.*

Sowerby, *loc. cit.*, p. 86, pl. xxii., figs. 39, 40.

Several small specimens were found alive under stones in the lagoon.

Smith unites* with this *L. basilanica* and *L. orientalis*, both of Adams and Reeve, and *L. fasciata*, Sowerby (not Linne).

LIMA FRAGILIS, *Gmelin.*

Sowerby, *loc. cit.*, p. 86, pl. xxii., figs. 34 – 37.

Small specimens were of frequent occurrence under stones in the lagoon.

Sowerby records this from Tahiti; Von Martens† from New Guinea and the Gilberts; and Smith‡ from Port Essington, Port Molle, Torres Straits, and Fiji. It is in this Museum from New Caledonia and Queensland.

PECTEN SQUAMATUS, *Gmelin.*

Reeve, Conch. Icon., viii., 1853, pl. xxi., fig. 82.

A few broken valves were collected on the beach of the lagoon.

---

* Smith—Chal. Rep., Zool., xiii., 1885, p. 289.
† Von Martens—Journ. Linn. Soc., Zool., xxi., 1889, p. 202.
‡ Smith—Zool. Coll. "Alert," 1884, p. 116.

PECTEN PALLIUM, *Linne.*

Reeve, *loc. cit.*, pl. xvii., fig. 63.

One valve from the lagoon beach.

This species appears to be widespread through the tropical Pacific. Cuming found it at Marutea, Paumotus. It is represented in this Museum from San Christoval, Solomons; Erromanga, New Hebrides; New Caledonia; Tonga; and the Gilberts.

P. novæ-guineæ, T. Woods, a Pleistocene fossil from Hall Sound, British New Guinea, is reduced to a synonym of *P. pallium* by Prof. R. Tate.

PECTEN DISTANS, *Reeve.*

Kobelt, Conch. Cab., Pecten, 1885, p. 228, pl. xli., fig. 2.

One valve from the lagoon beach.

New Caledonian specimens occur in the Museum series.

PECTEN MADREPORARUM, *Sowerby*

Sowerby, Thesaurus Conch., i., 1847, p. 68, pl. xiv., fig. 68.

One specimen from the lagoon beach.

Also represented in the Museum from Hood Lagoon and Tupuselei, British New Guinea; Cape York, Queensland; and New Caledonia. This species appears to be universally but erroneously ascribed to Petit. It is a perverse fate which credits an author, who was the first to energetically protest against manuscript names,[†] with indulging in the practice himself. Sowerby's locality, the Red Sea, as well as his authority, requires confirmation.

HINNITES, sp.

Attached to sheets of dead coral, and associated with the Brachiopod *Thecidea maxilla*, were several adherent valves of a species of *Hinnites*, too imperfect for specific determination.

PTERIA PEASEI, *Dunker.*

Dunker, Conch. Cab., Avicula, 1872, p. 24, pl. viii., fig. 1.

Attached (as mentioned *ante* p. 308) in great numbers to the branches of *Plexaura antipathes.*

The species was described by Pease[‡] under the thrice pre-occupied name of *Avicula radiata*, from the Gilberts. Schmeltz, who considers *A. cypsellus*, Dunker, a synonym,[§] reports it from Samoa.

PTERIA CUMINGII, *Reeve.*

Reeve, Conch. Icon. x., 1857, Avicula, pl. iv., sp. 6.

---

* Tate—Proc. Linn. Soc. N.S.W. (2), ix., 1894, p. 214.
† Petit—Revue Zool., ii., 1839, p. 346, and iii., 1840, p. 154.
‡ Pease—Proc. Zool. Soc., 1862, p. 244.
§ Schmeltz—Mus. Godeffroy Cat., v., 1874, p. 176.

This species is employed on Funafuti in the manufacture of fish-hooks (*ante* p. 268). I purchased a valve from a native on Nukulailai.

Cuming procured the type at Marutea, Paumotus.

MELINA SAMOENSIS, *Baird*.

Baird, in Brenchley, Cruise of the "Curaçoa," 1873, p. 454, pl. xlii., fig. 8.

Common ; attached to the under surfaces of coral blocks on the ocean beach of Funafuti, at low water. My specimens exceed the type in size, being upwards of 50 mm. in length.

I suspect that the prior *P. linguæformis*, Reeve, from the Society Islands, is but a depauperated form of this. The "Challenger" collected *M. samoensis* on the reefs at Honolulu and Hawaii ; the type came from Tutuila, Samoa.

Both Meek and Dall have pointed out* that the name of *Perna* must be superseded by that of *Melina*.

PINNA, sp.

Some fragments of a *Pinna*, perhaps *P. trigonalis*, Pease, were seen on the lagoon beach of Funafuti.

OSTREA HANLEYANA, *Sowerby*.

Sowerby, Conch. Icon., xviii., 1871, Ostrea, Pl. xxviii., sp. 72.

An oyster which occurred under stones beside *M. samoensis* is with much doubt so identified.

OSTREA CRISTAGALLI, *Linne*.

Sowerby, *loc. cit.*, pl. xi., sp. 22.

Obtained in eighteen fathoms, three miles south-west of the village (*ante* p. 328).

I collected this at Port Moresby, British New Guinea. It is represented in this Museum from Florida, Solomons ; Havannah Harbour, New Hebrides ; and Ouven, Loyalties.

CARDITA SWEETI, sp. nov.

(Fig. 50).

Shell solid, oblong, slightly oblique, inequilateral, little inflated. Colour dull white, upon the beak pale yellow. Sculptured by about forty-five close, raised, radiating ribs, separated by deep interstices a quarter of their width. In the median area the rays are smaller and closer together than at the sides, while at the extremities they rapidly enlarge and rather recurve. Upon

---

* Meek—Report U.S. Geol. Survey Territories, ix., 1876, p. 28, note ; Dall—Trans. Wagner Free Inst. Sci., iii., 1898, p. 665.

the rays are crowded small transverse lunate gemmules. Lunule sharply impressed, narrow, lanceolate. Ligament large, external.

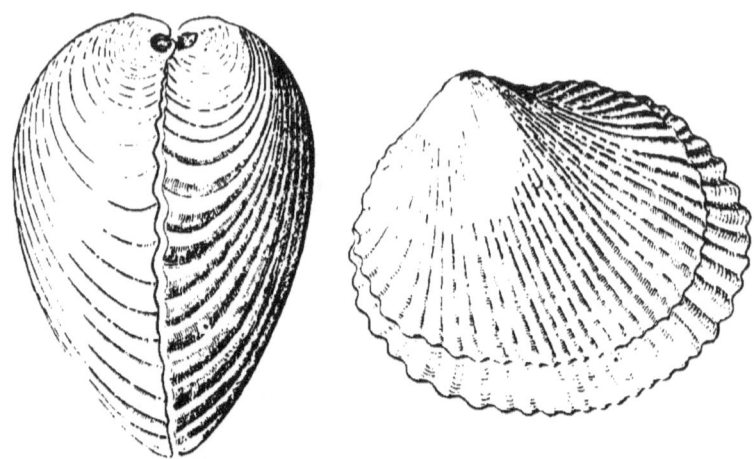

Fig. 50.

Hinge line short, straight, remainder of the margin evenly rounded. Internal margin sharply, finely crenulated. Length 14, breadth 12, diameter of conjoined valves 8 mm.

Fig. 50.

One entire shell, described above, was taken by Mr. G. Sweet; and a single, worn, slightly larger valve, by myself at Funafuti.

This species seems nearest to *C. dilecta*, Smith, but is distinguished from that and other members of the genus by more numerous ribs bearing closer packed grains.

The specific name is in compliment to Mr. G. Sweet, the finder, who was a member of the second expedition to Funafuti.

The side view is drawn to a smaller scale than the other sketches.

LUCINA EXASPERATA, *Reeve.*

Reeve, Conch. Icon., vi., 1850, Lucina, pl. i., sp. 4.

A few specimens from the lagoon.

Melvill and Standen notice this from Lifu. It is in this Museum from New Caledonia.

LUCINA PUNCTATA, *Linne.*

Pfeiffer, Conch. Cab., Veneracea, 1869, p. 262, pl. xix., figs. 8, 9.

One specimen from the lagoon beach.

Reported by Schmeltz from Samoa, Fiji, and Rarotonga; by Melvill and Standen from Lifu; and represented in this Museum from New Caledonia.

LUCINA DIVERGENS, *Philippi*.

Reeve, Conch. Icon., vi., 1850, Lucina, pl. vii., spp. 33, 37, 38.

Common on the lagoon beach.

Prof. von Martens has pointed out[*] that Philippi's name enjoys two month's priority over the better known *L. fibula*, of Reeve. He refers to it from Samoa and Fiji, and Melvill and Standen from Lifu. Material in this Museum show it to extend south along the Australian coast to Newcastle, New South Wales, and also to the Ladrones, New Hebrides, and New Caledonia.

LUCINA OBLONGA, sp. nov.
(Fig. 51).

Shell small, but thick and strong, ovate, very inequilateral, inflated. Colour, one specimen is white, the other pink. Sculpture —the umbones are smooth, the remainder closely and rather

Fig. 51.

irregularly covered with numerous, raised, strong, concentric, ribs, narrower than their interstices; faint radiating sculpture is barely visible in these interstices. Beaks prominent and much incurved. Lunule large, sharply impressed, sculptured by a faint continuation of the concentric ribs. Dorsal surface wanting the depression which characterises *L. seminula* and its allies. Interiorly the margin is most minutely crenulated. Length 3; height 3·75 mm.

Two valves from the lagoon beach.

Allied to *L. congenita*, Smith,[†] from which it differs by being narrower in proportion to height, more densely ribbed, and more inequilateral.

CORBIS FIMBRIATA, *Linne*.

Sowerby, Conch. Icon., xviii., 1872, Corbis, pl. i., sp. 1.

A living specimen occurred under blocks of coral in the lagoon.

Schmeltz quotes this from Fiji and the Pelews; Melvill and Standen from Lifu. It is in this Museum from Port Curtis, Queensland; New Caledonia; and Tonga.

---

[*] Von Martens—Journ. Linn. Soc., Zool., xxi., 1889, p. 209.
[†] Smith—Chall. Rep., Zool., xiii., 1885, p. 182, pl. xiii., figs. 7, 7a.

CRYPTODON GLOBOSUM, *Forskal*.

Reeve, Conch. Icon., vi., 1850, pl. v., sp. 21 (as *L. ovum*).

Common as dead shells on the lagoon beach.

Ranges along the east Australian coast south to St. Vincent's Gulf. Is represented in this Museum from Tonga.

TELLINA RUGOSA, *Born*.

Sowerby, Conch. Icon., xvii., Tellina, 1866, pl. ix., sp. 36.

A few dead, subfossil valves were picked up around the raised *Heliopora* reef.

Reported by H. Cuming from Rapa, Austral Islands ; by Melvill and Standen from Lifu ; and by Schmeltz from Samoa, Fiji, Rarotonga, and Tahiti. In this Museum it is represented from Moreton Bay, Queensland ; Pipon Islands, New Caledonia ; Tonga ; and Hawaii.

TELLINA SCOBINATA, *Linne*.

Sowerby, *loc. cit.*, pl. xiv., sp. 64.

Common on the lagoon beach.

Sowerby notes this from the Society Islands : Schmeltz from Samoa, Fiji, and Rarotonga ; Melvill and Standen from Lifu. This Museum contains it from the Solomons, Gilberts, and Tonga.

TELLINA FLAMMULA, *Deshayes*.

Sowerby, *loc cit.*, pl. lii, sp. 310.

A few valves from the lagoon beach.

Included in the Museum collection from Woodlark Island and New Caledonia.

TELLINA DISPAR, *Conrad*.

Sowerby, *loc. cit.*, pl. iii., sp. 10.

A few separate valves were noticed on the lagoon beach.

First described from Hawaii : noted by Schmeltz from Upolu and Tahiti ; and by Melvill and Standen from Lifu. Represented in this Museum from Port Curtis and Moreton Bay, Queensland ; and New Caledonia.

TELLINA OBLIQUARIA, *Deshayes*.

Sowerby, *loc. cit.*, pl. liv., sp. 321.

Several specimens from the beach of the lagoon, some rose, others lemon, others again lemon with rose stripes from the umbo.

Deshayes, in his original description,* records this species from the Pacific Ocean. Sowerby, in the reference quoted above,

---

* Deshayes—Proc. Zool. Soc., 1854, p. 356.

though actually mentioning the page of his predecessor's work, states that the habitat of the species is unknown. Such evidence of carelessness supports me in concluding that Sowerby again described this species as *T. obliquistriata,** from "Kingsmill Island," by which the Kingsmill or Gilbert Group are doubtless intended. It is in this Museum from Aneiteum, New Hebrides.

TELLINA RHOMBOIDES, *Quoy & Gaimard.*

Smith, Chall. Rep., Zool., xiii., 1885, p. 103.

Abundant in the lagoon.

Reported by Smith, under various names, from Guam in the Ladrones; Cape York, Queensland; and Levuka, Fiji; and by Melvill and Standen from Lifu. It is in this Museum from Aneiteum, New Hebrides.

TELLINA ROBUSTA, *Hanley.*

Sowerby, *loc. cit.*, pl. xvi., sp. 77.

. The yellow variety occurred in profusion in the lagoon.

Hanley reports this from Anaa, Paumotus; Schmeltz from Tahiti, Rarotonga, and Upolu. I have taken it at Hyenghien, New Caledonia. There are examples in the Museum from the Isle of Pines.

TELLINA OPALINA, *Sowerby.*

(Fig. 52).

Sowerby, *loc. cit.*, pl. xliv., sp. 258.

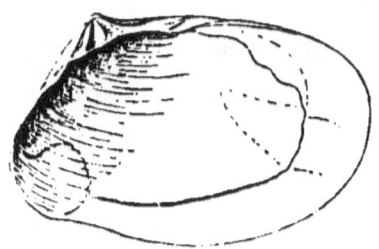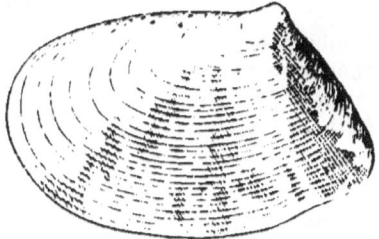

The paucity of information given by Sowerby permits no accurate determination, but suggests this name for a species of which I took a dozen odd valves on the beach of the lagoon. The species in question is in length 5·5, and in height 3·7 mm.; very glossy, radiately marked with translucent and opaque lines or dashes, the concentric sculpture almost effaced.

The original description gave no locality. Melvill and Standen supply† Madras and the Moluccas.

---

* Sowerby—Conch. Icon., xvii., 1866, pl. xliv., sp. 256.
† Melvill and Standen—Journ. Conch., ix., 1898, p. 85.

TELLINA FIJIENSIS, *Sowerby*.

Smith, *loc. cit.*, p. 107.

A few separate valves from the lagoon beach.

Previously reported from Marutea, Paumotus; and Ngau and Levuka, Fiji.

TELLINA CREBRIMACULATA, *Sowerby*.

Sowerby, *loc. cit.*, pl. li., sp. 301.

A few separate valves from the lagoon beach.

Hitherto only recorded from Fiji.

TELLINA ELLICENSIS, sp. nov.
(Fig. 53).

Shell small, very solid, opaque, very inequilateral, rather inflated anteriorly, height two-thirds of the length, truncate posteriorly. Colour white, irregularly painted with small rose spots and streaks. Sculptured over the entire surface by fine, close, concentric threads.

 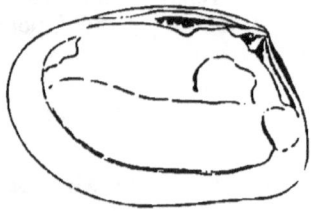

Fig. 53.

Umbo prominent. Fold almost obsolete. Dorsal margin straight, then curved anteriorly. Anterior margin curved the third of a circle. Ventral margin nearly straight, scarcely sinuated by the fold. Hinge composed of two cardinal teeth, a strong anterior lateral and a weaker posterior lateral tooth. Length 6, height 4 mm.

This species is allied by sculpture and contour to *T. tenuilirata*, Sowerby, from which a much shorter, broader outline clearly separates it.

One right valve was found on the beach of the Funafuti lagoon.

LIBITINA GUINAICA, *Lamarck*.

Reeve, Conch. Icon., i., Cypricardia, 1843, pl. ii., species 13.

Plentiful dead on the beaches; once found alive in a crevice in a block of coral in the lagoon.

The only other Pacific record seems to be the finding of it by Hugh Cuming at Marutea, Paumotus.

CIRCE PECTINATA, *Linne.*

Römer, Mon. Veneridæ, i., 1869, p. 174, pl. xlvii, figs. 1a–d.

Common in the Funafuti lagoon ; collected alive among loose rocks.

Römer quotes this from Marutea, Paumotus ; Fischer from New Caledonia ; Schmeltz from Bowen, and Smith from Thursday Island, Queensland. It is in this Museum from Fiji ; Port Moresby, British New Guinea ; and Port Curtis, Queensland.

CIRCE PICTA, *Lamarck.*

Römer, *loc. cit.,* p. 164, pl. xlv., fig. 3.

Two valves from the lagoon beach.

Smith states* that the distinction between this and several admitted species is obscure. Schmeltz quotes it from Upolu, Samoa ; and Melvill and Standen from Lifu.

CIRCE CASTRENSIS, *Linne.*

Römer, *loc. cit.,* p. 159, pl. xliv.

A few valves were found on the lagoon beach.

Smith has recorded this from Bowen, Queensland. In this Museum it is represented from New Caledonia ; the Loyalties ; Aneiteum, New Hebrides ; Guadalcanar, Solomons ; and Tonga-tabu, Tonga.

CYTHEREA OBLIQUATA, *Hanley,* var. PRORA, *Conrad.*

Römer, *loc. cit.,* p. 107, pl. xxix., fig. 1, pl. xxxiii., figs. 4, 5.

Very common on the lagoon beach.

Schmeltz quotes this from Fiji, Tahiti, and Rarotonga. The Museum series show it from Port Curtis, Queensland ; and New Caledonia.

CYTHEREA SUBPELLUCIDA, *Sowerby.*

Römer, *loc. cit.,* p. 112, pl. xxx., fig. 4.

One specimen from the lagoon beach.

VENUS TOREUMA, *Gould.*

Reeve, Conch. Icon., xiv., 1863, Venus, pl. xvi., sp. 64.

Several valves from the lagoon beach.

Smith records this from Port Molle and Port Curtis, Queensland. Other Queensland localities shown by the Museum collection are Torres Straits, Bowen, and Moreton Bay.

* Smith—*Loc. cit.,* p. 146.

Venus puerpera, *L.*, var. listeri, *Gray.*

Reeve, *loc. cit.*, pl. v., sp. 14.

Several adult valves were taken on the lagoon beach ; and what seems a very young shell was caught by the tangles in forty to eighty fathoms on the western slope of the atoll.

Venerupis macrophylla, *Deshayes.*

Sowerby, Thes. Conch., ii., 1855, p. 763, pl. clxv., fig. 20.

One small specimen taken boring dead coral in the lagoon.

Naranio lapicida, *Chemnitz.*

Sowerby, Thes. Conch., ii., 1855, p. 776, pl. clxvi., fig. 26.

Found boring loose coral blocks in the lagoon.

Schmeltz quotes this from Yap, Pelews. Sowerby mentions it from Australia ; though no doubt it occurs on the Great Barrier Reef, I am not acquainted with Australian examples of the typical form with posterior radiating ribs. A thinner, smoother form, (var. *divaricata*) has been noticed in South Australia. A useful index to the genus is given by Tryon.*

Kellia pacifica, sp. nov.
(Fig. 54).

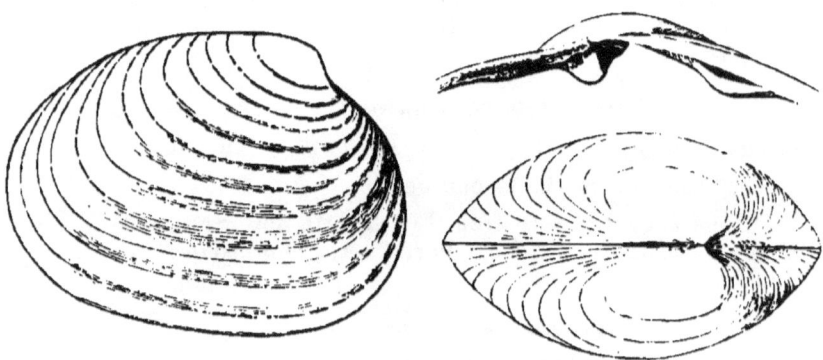

Fig. 54.

Shell oblong, inflated, most glossy, iridescent by reflected light. Equivalve, margins closed. Inequilateral to the extent of the posterior being twice the length of the anterior. Colour milky on the umbones, cream on the ventral margins, with concentric opaque and translucent zones. Sculptured by delicate unequal growth lines which grow coarser with age. Beaks small, almost touching, forwardly directed. Ventral margin straight, anteriorly truncated, posterior rounded and dorsal gently curved.

* Tryon—Am. Journ. Conch., vii., 1872, p. 258.

Length 11, height 8, breadth of conjoined valves 5·5 mm.

Alive in the lagoon under loose blocks of dead coral. There is a specimen of this species in this Museum from New Caledonia, labelled by Mr. E. A. Smith, "*Scintilla ovulina*, Desh.," with the description and figure of which it does not agree.

SCINTILLA SEMICLAUSA, *Sowerby*.

Sowerby, Conch. Icon., xix., Scintilla, 1874, pl. ii., sp. 9.

One specimen alive in shallow water in the lagoon.

Recorded by Melvill and Standen from Lifu.

ATACTODEA STRIATA, *Gmelin*.
(Fig. 55).

Reeve, Conch. Icon., viii., Mesodesma, 1854, pl. ii., sp. 10.

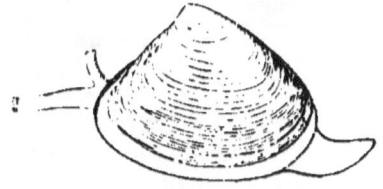

Abundant alive in sand at low water along the margin of the lagoon. It was eaten by the children who called it "assouri." An enlarged drawing taken from life on the spot is here reproduced. The animal is extremely bold and active, it is cream colour with a vivid scarlet border to the anterior edge of the mantle.

Fig. 55.

Unless slight difference of sculpture be regarded as of specific distinction, this species is shown by Museum material, under various names from Port Curtis, Eclipse Island, Queensland; Guam, Ladrones; Teste Island, Louisiade Archipelago; the Solomons; New Hebrides; Fiji; and Samoa.

ASAPHIS DEFLORATA, *Linne*.

Reeve, Conch. Icon., x., Capsa, 1856, pl. i.

This species is abundant on the Funafuti lagoon.

Reeve reports it from Tahiti, and Melvill and Standen from Lifu. It is represented in this Museum from Torres Straits and Port Curtis, Queensland; Woodlark Island, British New Guinea; Vate, New Hebrides; New Caledonia; and the Gilberts.

PSAMMOBIA SQUAMOSA, *Lamarck*.

Reeve, Conch. Icon., x., 1857, Psammobia, pl. vii., sp. 50.

One young and separate valve from the lagoon beach.

CARDIUM ANGULATUM, *Lamarck*.

Reeve, Conch. Icon., ii., 1845, Cardium, pl. xiv., sp. 70.

Single valves are not uncommon on the lagoon beaches.

Specimens of this species are contained in this Museum from New Caledonia and Uea or Wallis Island. It is represented by the above quoted illustration, and is also identical with specimens returned from the British Museum under the name of "*Cardium philippinense*, Deshayes"; this name I have been unable to trace in literature.

CARDIUM MACULOSUM, *Wood.*

Reeve, *loc. cit.*, pl. xvi., sp. 76.

A few separate valves were found on the lagoon beach.

CARDIUM CARDISSA, var. DIONÆUM, *Sowerby.*

Reeve, *loc. cit.*, pl. xxi., sp. 122.

Common on the lagoon beach.

This was first collected by Cuming on Anaa, Paumotus.

CARDIUM FRAGRUM, *Linne.*

Reeve, *loc. cit.*, pl. iv., sp. 23.

Common in the lagoon.

It is represented in this Museum from Port Curtis, Queensland, and New Caledonia.

C. FRAGRUM, var. SUEZIENSE, *Issel.*

Smith, Chall. Rep., Zool., xiii., 1885, p. 158, pl. viii., figs. 2, 2a, 2b.

Separate valves were abundant on the lagoon beach, and one was obtained outside the atoll at a depth of eighty to forty fathoms.

The four dozen odd valves before me exhibit much variation in contour, and they appear to pass by gradual transition into typical *C. fragrum.* Smith, who redescribes and refigures the species, rests his definition chiefly on form. The figure of Issel,[*] which he condemns, can in outline be exactly matched by Funafuti material. Possibly the species tends in deeper water to assume this form. The "Challenger" dredged it off Fiji, and this Museum possesses examples from Torres Straits.

TRIDACNA GIGAS, *L.*, var. SQUAMOSA, *Lamarck.*

Reeve, Conch. Icon., xiv., Tridacna, 1862, pl. iii.

Not uncommon among the reefs of the lagoon.

Known to the natives of Funafuti as "Fasua tuka," (*ante* p. 67) and by them, as by other South Sea Islanders, esteemed for food.[†] It had a further economic value as material for ornaments and

---

[*] Issel—Malacologia del Mar Rosso, 1869, pl. iii., fig. 4.

[†] Hedley in Thomson—British New Guinea, 1892, p. 283.

axe heads.* The natives of the Solomon Islands prefer fossil to recent shells for this purpose.†

What information we have, suggests that the range of this species is almost co-extensive with that of the reef-building corals.

Weights and measures of sundry large individuals have lately been published by Smith,‡ his maximum record being five hundred and seven pounds weight, and fifty-four inches in length. This is almost reached by an unquoted record from the Isle of Pines, New Caledonia. Dr. T. Mialaret writes§:—"In the middle of the peninsula which encloses the Bay of Oupi on the east, there occurs, sunk in the coral, the edges of its valves level with the surface of the rock, a gigantic *Tridacna* measuring at least 1 metre 20 in length. At the request of Admiral Courbet, we attempted in 1882 to extract it, but all our efforts were in vain."

The genus *Tridacna* appears to suffer from a superfluity of specific names. No characters of permanent value separate *T. squamosa* from *T. gigas*. These forms are usually if not invariably free.‖ On the contrary, the habit of *T. elongata* is to bury itself in rock, a habit always causing variability in shape.

Hanley states that it was upon what Lamarck called " *T. squamosa* " that Linne himself founded his *Chama gigas*.¶

Tridacna elongata, *Lamarck*.

Reeve, *loc. cit.*, pl. ii. ; Valliant, Ann. Sci. Nat., iv., 1865, pp. 65 – 172, pls. viii. – xii.

This species is abundant, perforating dead coral in the Funafuti lagoon. So firmly does the foot adhere, that when wrenching the shell out of its burrow, I have sometimes torn the animal asunder, leaving the foot attached to the rock. The position of the shells embedded in dead coral is well displayed in one of W. S. Kent's photographs.**

·The natives, who distinguish it from the preceding as " Fasua noa," also use it as food.

The range of *T. elongata* appears to exceed that of *T. gigas*, the furthest southern point reached by it in the Pacific being Lord Howe Island.

---

* Valliant—Bull. Soc. Geol. Fr., xxv., 1868, pp. 681 – 687.
† Willey—*Nature*, Oct. 1896, p. 523.
‡ Smith—Proc. Malac. Soc., iii., 1898, p. 112.
§ Mialaret—L'Ile des Pins, son Passé, son Present, son Avenir, 1897, p. 63.
    Kent—Great Barrier Reef, 1893, pp. 44–45, pl. xxix.
¶ Hanley—Ipsa Linnæi Conchylia, 1855, p. 85.
** Kent—*Loc. cit.*, foreground of No. 1, pl. iv.

CHAMA IMBRICATA, *Broderip*.

Broderip, Trans. Zool. Soc., 1835, p. 304, pl. xxxix., fig. 2; Lischke, Jap. Meeres Conch., ii., 1871, p. 126, pl. ix., fig. 4.

Chama foliacea, Quoy and Gaimard, Voy. "Astrolabe," Zool., iii., 1835, p. 478, pl. lxxviii., fig. 19.

Abundant at low water in the Funafuti lagoon, a mile south of the village.

The foliations on the opercular valve are in my specimens all worn away, and for identification I have relied on the contour, the dark purple stain on the upper interior margin, and the absence of marginal crenulations. The *C. foliacea*, Q. & G., from Vanikoro, appears to me to be identical. As Broderip's preliminary description* did not appear till April 3rd, 1835,† I do not know whether it was in London or in Paris that the species was first published.

Hugh Cuming brought the type from Marutea, Paumotus; Melvill and Standen note it from Lifu. An example from Anciteum, New Hebrides, is in this Museum.

CHAMA SPINOSA, *Broderip*.

Broderip, *loc. cit.*, p. 306, pl. xxxviii., figs. 8, 9.

Two specimens from the lagoon.

If I have correctly identified this species, the upper valve must have always been wrongly drawn. In a specimen before me, the umbo is at a third of the diameter of the valve from the hinge, and around it the valve has performed three spiral volutions.

Found by Cuming at Marutea, Paumotus.

CHAMA UNICORNIS, *Bruguiere*.

Clessin, Conch. Cab., Chama, 1888, p. 15, pl. ii., figs. 3, 4.

With doubt I so identify, from insufficient figures and description, a specimen with two revolutions, 15 mm. long from Funafuti.

CORBULA TAHEITENSIS, *Lamarck*.

Reeve, Conch. Icon., ii., Corbula, 1843, pl. ii., sp. 15.

One of the most abundant shells on the lagoon beach, but I did not meet with it alive.

To the original locality of Tahiti, Smith adds that of New Guinea.‡

GASTROCHÆNA LAMELLOSA, *Deshayes*.

Smith, Chall. Rep., Zool., xiii., 1885, p. 28, pl. vii., figs. 2, 2b.

Found alive, boring in coral blocks, in the lagoon.

* Broderip—Proc. Zool. Soc., 1834, p. 149.
† See Sclater—Proc. Zool. Soc., 1894, p. 436.
‡ Smith—Proc. Zool. Soc., 1891, p. 430.

Smith reports this from Torres Straits. In this Museum it is represented from Fiji; New Caledonia; Moreton Bay, Queensland: and St. Vincent's Gulf, South Australia.

NAUSITORIA AURITA, sp. nov.
(Fig. 56).

Shell distinguished by an auricle which is much recurved outwards and above; within, it is raised above the surface of the valve. This character is illustrated by Fig. 56, showing exterior and interior of the right valve. Ventral or median area rather broad. Apophyses short and broad. Hinge tubercle bifid. Length 9, breadth 9 mm. Palettes unknown.

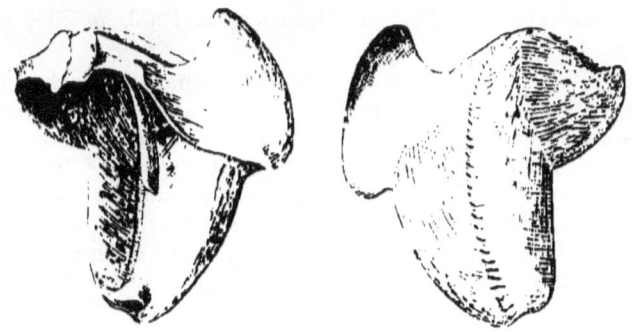

Fig 56.

A log, recognised by a bushman of our party as kauri (*ante* p. 40) which came ashore at Funafuti, had been bored by this mollusc. On breaking the wood up with an axe, I found the only vestiges left of the animal to be a pair of valves broken at the ventral tips, which I found in a burrow.

Mr. R. C. Rossiter afterwards generously presented me with a couple of perfect valves, specifically identical with these Funafuti shells, which he collected at Noumea, New Caledonia.

An ally of this seems to be a species of unknown origin named by Sowerby *Teredo campanulata*, that is however apparently narrower in the ventral portion, and even more produced and recurved in the auricle.

I recently examined[*] certain Australian shipworms, and remarked that they differed from *Teredo* generically. For their reception I selected the genus *Calobates*, Gould (1862), revised the characters of that genus, and subordinated to it *Nausitoria*, Wright (1864), and *Lyrodus*, Gould (1870). It unfortunately escaped my attention that Tapparone Canefri had already pointed out[†] that *Calobates*, as a generic term, had been twice preoccupied

* Hedley—Proc. Linn. Soc. N.S.W., xxiii., 1898, p. 91.
† Tapparone Canefri—Ann. Mus. Civ. Genoa, ix., 1877, p. 290.

for birds, and was therefore inadmissible. He proposed to sub-
stitute *Bactronophorus*, Tapparone Canefri (1877). As, however,
the prior name of *Nausitoria* is available, that must come into
use when *Calobates* is abandoned.

The Teredinidæ have been unfortunate in their monographers.
The account in the last volume of the Conchologia Iconia, by
Sowerby, is a slovenly production and full of errors. Even worse
is an alleged Monograph by Clessin in the Conchylien Cabinet,
of which the text and illustrations disgrace that serial. The
latter memoir is absolutely the worst zoological monograph I have
read.

POROMYA GRANULATA, *Nyst & Westendrop.*

Forbes and Hanley, British Mollusca, i., 1853, p. 204, pl. ix.,
figs. 4 – 6.

A single valve was collected on the Funafuti beach, which I
refer with doubt to this species. It is more oblong than the
figure quoted, but as I have no authentic specimen for comparison,
and as Dall credits this species with great variation* in form and
sculpture, I refrain from assigning specific value to the apparent
difference. According to this writer, *P. australis*, Smith,† from
Cape York, Queensland, is but a variety. The difference between
this and such a figure as that of Sars‡ is great enough to include
the form before me.

BRACHIOPODA.

THECIDEA MAXILLA, sp. nov.
(Fig. 57.)

Shell small, of variable contour, somewhat boat shaped, attached
to stones, shells, or the like, by the beak of the pedicle valve.
Colour, dull pale yellow. Sculpture—both valves marked by
delicate concentric growth lines and microscopically shagreened.
Length of a large specimen, 6 mm. ; breadth 3½ mm.

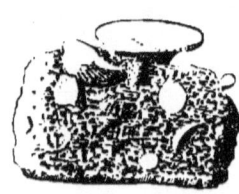

Fig. 57.

Pedicle valve deep, hinge line straight,
cardinal area triangular, apex rather recurved. Margin finely granulate, frequently
emarginate in front. Protruding from beneath the hinge are two slender prongs
arising from a deep seated septum. External
to these, and just beneath the hinge line, are
two heavy, projecting, wedge-shaped cardinal teeth. The interior of the valve is
irregularly studded with sharp points and
tubercles arranged longitudinally, and varying in different individuals.

---

* Dall—Bull. Mus. Comp. Zool., xii., 1886, p. 282.
† Smith—Chall. Rep., Zool., xiii., 1885, p. 54, pl. xi., figs. 2, 2a, 2b.
‡ Sars—Mollusca regionis Articæ Norvegiæ, 1878, pl. v., figs. 6a, 6b.

The brachial valve is externally horse-shoe shaped, and has a slight median boss. Internally it has a straight hinge line, from beneath which and in the plane of the valve, projects a stout cardinal process, whose transverse vertical section would form an omega, hollow downwards. On either side of the cardinal process, and corresponding to the teeth of the lower valve, are two deep triangular impressions, the sockets. All the free edge of the upper valve is granulated. The frontal emargination gradually passes into a funnel directed backwards; here originates the median septum which tapers distally to an acicular point before the hinge. The ventral face of the septum is hollow, on the right and left of it are produced curled flanges with serrate edges. These edges vary much; in some, presumably old, individuals they project irregular jagged lobes into the cavity.

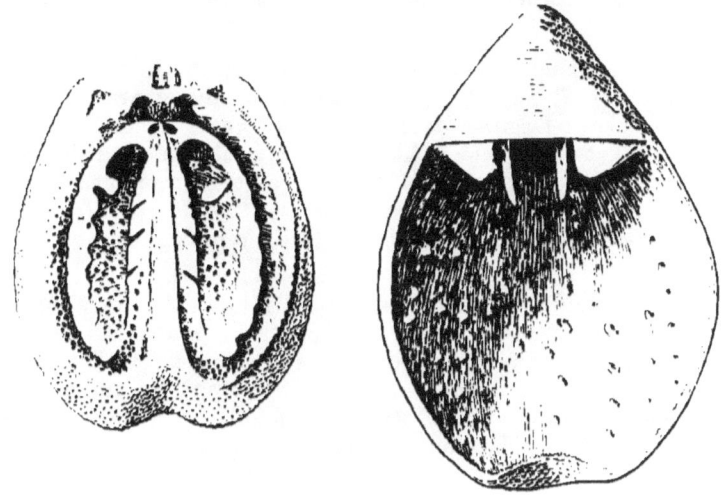

Fig. 57.

If this median septum be compared to the tongue, then the teeth of the human jaw would answer in position to the lateral lobes of the brachial lamellæ. Their development varies much; what I take to be a young stage is shown in my drawing. In other, presumedly aged examples, the "canines" and "molars" project as tusks sideways and downwards, while the "incisors" coalesce and advance towards the hinge. The cavity of the valve, exclusive of the septum and lamellæ, has the surface densely perforated.

This species was attached in considerable numbers, horizontally, perpendicularly, or obliquely (Fig. 57) to loose sheets of dead coral which I pulled up by tangles in forty to eighty fathoms on the western slope of Funafuti. At first inspection I mistook them for the young of a *Spondylus*, hence the erroneous statement on p. 402, that the Brachiopoda were absent from the Archipelago.

The genus *Thecidea* dates back from the opening of the Mesozoic, and is manifested in numerous species through a long range of formations. Like *Nautilus* and *Trigonia*, it now only survives in a few rare and restricted species. It is an interesting coincidence that a genus so intimately associated with fossil coral reefs in Europe, should recur alive on a Pacific Atoll. So far but two recent species, *T. mediterranea*, Risso, and *T. barretti*, Woodward, have been detected. The former, for which the subgenus *Lacazella* has been proposed by Munier Chalmas, is unlike the Pacific species; whereas the latter and the West Indian *T. barretti* are quite close. These conform neither to *Thecidea*, as restricted by Hall and Clarke,* nor to the various subgenera admitted by them. That generic term has been here used in the wider application of Davidson.

On comparing examples of *T. maxilla* with the published accounts of *T. barretti*, I conclude that the characters are so variable that a large series of each will be necessary to discriminate properly between them. At present I would point to the flanges of the median septum and to the greater development of the brachial lamellæ, as features possessed by *T. maxilla* but not by *T. barretti*.† The former, indeed, reminds one of a split walnut.

I am in doubt whether a pseudo-deltidium exists in *T. barretti*, for Davidson writes‡ that "in external shape it cannot be distinguished from the Mediterranean species," which has the pseudo-deltidium; and in a small drawing§ he indicates the pseudo-deltidium. But, on the other hand, in the enlarged drawing,‖ on which I place more reliance, it is not depicted. Again, it is not shown in his first illustration,¶ nor is it mentioned in either description. Should a pseudo-deltidium be absent in *T. barretti*, as it certainly is in *T. maxilla*, that would isolate these two from the remainder of the genus.

Another feature in common is the fork which projects in two slender prongs between the cardinal teeth in both species, and strikingly differs from the spoon-shaped processes of *T. mediterranea* and from the three prongs of *T. radiata*, the type of the genus.

---

* Hall and Clarke—47th Ann. Report New York State Mus., 1894, pp. 1091–1093.
† Dall—Bull. Mus. Comp. Zool., xii., 1886, pl. vi., fig. 2.
‡ Davidson—Trans. Linn. Soc., Zool. (2), iv., 1889, p. 162.
§ Davidson—*Loc. cit.*, pl. xxiii., fig. 9a.
‖ Davidson—*Loc. cit.*, pl. xxiii., fig. 10.
¶ Davidson—Geol. Mag., i., 1864, pl. ii., fig. 1a.

SUMMARY OF THE FAUNA OF FUNAFUTI.

XIX

SUMMARY OF THE FAUNA OF FUNAFUTI.

The fauna of the Atoll of Funafuti, as presented by different writers in the preceding pages, will now be briefly enumerated in systematic order. With that information will also be incorporated various records, either overlooked in the preparation of the articles referred to, or produced since their publication, and embracing the Archipelago as a whole.

Prior to the advent of the Expedition, not more than eight species of animals were recorded in literature from Funafuti ; the following lists embrace about eight hundred and fifty entries.

Though the student of Zoogeography will herein find a more complete account of the life of a Central Pacific Atoll than has previously appeared, he is cautioned not to use it as an exhaustive catalogue. The results of brief sojourn by a few poorly equipped visitors, may indeed present a picture in which the salient features loom obscurely, as in a partly-developed photograph, but nothing more.

Class MAMMALIA.

Mus exulans, *Peale*.   Delphinus, *sp*.

Class AVES.

The account of the Avifauna of the atoll by Mr. A. J. North (pp. 79 – 88) can be supplemented by a few additions. Dr. H. Gadow has briefly enumerated the birds shot on Funafuti by Mr. J. S. Gardiner.[*] To these he adds *Carpophaga pistrinaria*, a species identified on the wing by his informant. As Mr. Gardiner was not previously acquainted with this species, such an identification cannot be considered of value, and I accordingly exclude it. In 1897 Mr. W. G. Woolnough, B.Sc., succeeded in shooting an example of the much debated Ellice Island Pigeon, which was subsequently determined by Mr. A. J. North as *Globicera pacifica*.[†]

The avifauna of the Archipelago will doubtless be found on examination to contain most, if not all, of the twenty-six birds observed in the neighbouring Phœnix Group.[‡] At present the revised list drawn up by Mr. A. J. North, consists of the following fifteen species :—

---

[*] Gadow—Ibis (7), iv., Jan. 1898, p. 45.
[†] North—Rec. Aust. Mus., iii., June, 1898, p. 86.
[‡] Lister—Proc. Zool. Soc., 1891, p. 300.

Urodynamis taitensis, *Sparrmann*.
Fregata aquila, *Linne*.
Demiegretta sacra, *Gmelin*.
Globicera pacifica, *Gmelin*.
Charadrius fulvus, *Gmelin*.
Totanus incanus, *Gmelin*.
Numenius tahoiteneis, *Gmelin*.
Strepsilas interpres, *Linne*.
Limosa novæzealandiæ, *Gray*.
Anous stolidus, *Linne*.
Micranous leucocapillus, *Gould*.
Procelsterna caerulea, *Bennett*.
Sterna anaestheta, *Scopulinus*.
    ,,   melanauchen, *Temminck*.
Gygis candida, *Gmelin*.

Class REPTILIA.

Chelone mydas, *Linne*.
Gymnodactylus pelagicus, *Girard*.
Gehyra oceanica, *Lesson*.
Lygosoma cyanurum, *Lesson*.
    ,,   adspersum, *Steindachner*.

Class PISCES.

The following list includes the fishes of Funafuti as reported by Mr. E. R. Waite (*ante* pp. 181 – 201, and Supplement, *vide* Appendix). About a fifth of them appears in a list of fishes obtained at Rotuma by Mr. J. S. Gardiner.*

Epinephelus urodelus, *Cuvier and Valenciennes*.
    ,,   leopardus, *Lacépède*.
    ,,   tauvina, *Forskal*.
    ,,   merra, *Bloch*.
    ,,   fuscoguttatus, *Forskal*.
Grammistes sexlineatus, *Thunberg*.
Lutianus bengalensis, *Bloch*.
    ,,   gibbus, *Forskal*.
    ,,   fulviflamma, *Forskal*.
Zanclus cornutus, *Linne*.
Chætodon auriga, *Forskal*.
Mulloides flavolineatus, *Lacépède*.
    ,,   samoeusis, *Günther*.
Upeneus trifasciatus, *Lacépède*.
Lethrinus rostratus, *Cuvier and Valenciennes*.
    ,,   ramak, *Forskal*.
Sphærodou grandoculis, *Forskal*.
Cirrhites maculatus, *Lacépède*.

---

* Boulenger—Ann. Mag. Nat. Hist. (6), xx., 1897, pp. 371 – 4.

Holocentrum erythraeum, *Günther*.
  ,,   diploxiphus, *Günther*
Teuthis rostrata, *Cuvier and Valenciennes*.
Histiophorus *sp*.
Acanthurus triostegus, *Linne*.
  ,,   guttatus, *Forskal*.
  ,,   blochii, *Cuvier and Valenciennes*.
  ,,   achilles, *Shaw*.
Naseus lituratus, *Forskal*.
Caranx sanctæ helenæ, *Cuvier and Valenciennes*.
  ,,   crumenopthalmus, *Bloch*.
Chorinemus sancti-petri, *Cuvier and Valenciennes*.
Trachynotus baillonii, *Lacépède*.
Thynnus pelamys, *Linne*.
Ruvettus pretiosus, *Cocco*.
Echeneis naucrates, *Linne*.
Gobius biocellatus, *Cuvier and Valenciennes*.
Salarias marmoratus, *Bennett*.
  ,,   periopthalmus, *Cuvier and Valenciennes*.
  ,,   quadricornis, *Cuvier and Valenciennes*.
Sphyræna *sp*.
Myxus leuciscus, *Günther*.
Tetradrachmum aruanum, *Bloch*.
Glyphidodon brownriggii, *Bennett*.
  ,,   sordidus, *Forskal*.
  ,,   septum-fasciatus, *Cuvier and Valeciennesn*.
Chilinus trilobatus, *Lacépède*.
  ,,   fasciatus, *Bloch*.
Epibulus insidiator, *Pallas*.
Julis lunaris, *Linne*.
Pseudoscarus pulchellus, *Rüppell*.
  ,,   bataviensis, *Bleeker*.
  ,,   singapurensis, *Bleeker*.
  ,,   troschelli, *Bleeker*.
Fierasfer homii, *Richardson*.
Platophrys pantherinus, *Rüppell*.
Belone platura, *Bennett*.
Hemirhamphus balinensis, *Bleeker*.
Exocœtus *sp*.
Ophichthys colubrinus, *Boddaert*.
Murœna formosa, *Bleeker*.
  ,,   buroënsis, *Bleeker*.
Balistes fuscus, *Bloch*.
  · ,,   flavomarginatus, *Rüppell*.
  ,,   aculeatus, *Linne*.
Tetrodon nigropunctatus, *Bloch*.
  ,,   margaritatus, *Rüppell*.
  ,,   immaculatus, *Bloch*.
Dicotylichthys punctulatus, *Kaup*.

Carcharias lamia, *Risso.*
Galeocerdo rayneri, *M'Donald and Barron.*
Alopias vulpes, *Gmelin.*
Urogymnus asperrimus, *Bloch.*
Trygon *sp.*
Ceratoptera *sp.*

Class HEMICHORDA.

Ptychodera flava, *Eschscholtz.*
   ,,   hedleyi, *Hill.*

Class CRUSTACEA.

Since the issue of the foregoing part of this Memoir dealing with the Crustacea, there has appeared a valuable series of articles by Mr. L. A. Borradaile* on Crustacea from the South Pacific, including those taken on Funafuti by Mr. J. S. Gardiner.

Mr. Borradaile conjectures that as *Pagurus setifer* is so closely allied to *P. guttatus,* the record of the latter from Funafuti may be a case of mistaken identity. Mr. Whitelegge, on re-examination of the example in question, maintains that it cannot be *P. setifer,* inasmuch as, among other characters, the left leg of the third pair in the Funafuti crab is setiferous all round and without sculpture ; whereas both the description of Milne Edwards and the figure of Hilgendorf, confine the bristles to the margin of the leg of *P. setifer.* The identification was arrived at after comparison with examples of *P. setifer* from Mauritius and Fiji.

A *Lambrus* allied to *L. intermedius,* Miers, and possibly new, was dredged by Mr. G. Halligan at a depth of two hundred fathoms off Tutaga Islet, Funafuti.

A Cirriped, noted by Schmeltz from the Ellice,† *Lithothyra rhodiopus,* has also been included.

Lambrus *sp.*
Atergatis floridus, *Rumphius.*
Actæa rugata, *Adams and White.*
Xanthodes lamarckii, *Milne Edwards.*
   ,,   nitidulus, *Dana.*
Zozymus æneus, *Dana.*
Daira perlata, *Herbst.*
Etisus laevimanus, *Randall.*
Etisodes caelatus, *Dana.*
Carpilodes margaritatus, *Milne Edwards.*
Pilumnus vestitus, *Haswell.*
   ,,   prunosus, *Whitelegge.*

---

* Borradaile—Proc. Zool. Soc , 1898, pp 32 – 38, 457 – 468, 1000 – 1015; and Ann. Mag. Nat. Hist. (7), ii., 1898, pp. 376 – 391.

† Schmeltz—Cat. Mus. Godeff., v., 1874, p. 83.

Actaeodes speciosa, *Dana.*
Phymodius monticulosus, *Dana.*
Pseudozius caystrus, *Adams and White.*
Leptodius exaratus, *Milne Edwards.*
,, sanguineus, *Milne Edwards.*
Ruppellia annulipes, *Milne Edwards.*
Eriphia scabricula, *Dana*
,, laevimana, *Latreille.*
Trapezia cymodoce, *Herbst.*
,, ferruginea, *Latreille.*
Thalamita integra, *Dana.*
,, admete, *Herbst.*
Cardisoma hirtipes, *Dana.*
Ocypoda ceratophthalma, *Pallas.*
Gelasimus tetragonon, *Herbst.*
Metopograpsus messor, *Forskal.*
Grapsus maculatus, *Catesby.*
Geograpsus crinipes, *Dana.*
Leiolophus planissimus, *Herbst.*
Calappa hepatica, *Linne.*
Cryptodromia japonica, *Henderson.*
Remipes pacificus, *Dana.*
Birgus latro, *Linne.*
Cenobita olivieri, *Owen.*
,, clypeata, *Milne Edwards.*
,, perlata, *Milne Edwards.*
,, rugosa, *Milne Edwards.*
,, ,, var. pulchra, *Dana.*
Diogenes pallescens, *Whitelegge.*
Pagurus fabimanus, *Dana.*
,, setifer, *Milne Edwards.*
,, guttatus, *Olivier.*
,, euopsis, *Dana.*
Clibanarius virescens, *Dana.*
,, corallinus, *Milne Edwards*
Clibanarius aequabilis, *Dana*
,, zebra, *Dana.*
,, cruentatus, *Milne Edwards.*
Calcinus elegans, *Milne Edwards.*
,, gaimardi, *Milne Edwards.*
,, latens, *Randall.*
,, herbsti, *de Man.*
,, ,, var. lividus, *Milne Edwards.*
Aniculus typicus, *Fabricius.*
Galathea affinis, *Ortmann.*
Petrolisthes lamarckii, *Leach.*
,, ,, var. asiaticus, *Leach.*
,, ,, var. rufescens, *Heller.*
,, ,, var. fimbriatus, *Borradaile.*

Porcellana sollasi, *Whitelegge*.
Ibacus antarcticus, *Rumphius*.
Palinurus guttatus, *Latreille*.
Palæmonella tridentata, *Borradaile*.
Hippolyte gibberosus, *Milne Edwards*.
Saron marmoratus, *Olivier*.
Athanas sulcatipes, *Borradaile*.
Alphæus edwardsii, *Audouin*.
,, laevis, *Randall*.
,, strenuus, *Dana*.
,, parvirostris, *Dana*.
,, collumianus, *Stimpson*.
,, frontalis, *Say*.
,, prolificus, *Bate*.
,, funafutensis, *Borradaile*.
Betacus minutus, *Whitelegge*.
Periclimenes danae, *Stimpson*.
Coralliocaris brevirostris, *Borradaile*.
Anchistus miersi, *de Man*.
Callianidea typa, *Milne Edwards*.
Gondactylus chiragra, *Fabricius*.
Pseudosquilla ciliata, *Fabricius*.
Cirolana latystylis, *Dana*.
Athelgue aniculi, *Whitelegge*.
Lithotrya nicobarica, *Reinhardt*.
,, rhodiopus, *Gray*.

Class Arachnida.

Since the publication of the preceding account (pp. 89 – 124) of the Spiders and Insects of Funafuti, Mr. R. I. Pocock has dealt with the series simultaneously collected by Messrs. Sollas and Gardiner, which embraced forms not procured by Mr. Hedley.* Mr. Pocock differs from Mr. Rainbow in sundry matters of species and genera. In the determination of the Scorpion, the latter accepts his correction, but he maintains the specific status of the various Spiders disputed by Mr. R. I. Pocock. Though the two names, *Obisium antipodum*, Simon, and *Olpium longiventer*, Keyserling, probably refer to one species, both provisionally appear in the following list. This under Mr. Rainbow's guidance, has been compiled from the two articles mentioned. It therefore represents his latest opinion on the subject. Included are also the Lepidoptera previously recorded from the Archipelago by Butler; two beetles, *Ceresium simplex* and *Sphenophorus obscurus*, taken by Mr. A. E. Finckh on Funafuti, in 1898; and a series of ants, noted from the Ellice by Mayr.† One of the new beetles discovered at

---

* R. I. Pocock—Ann. Mag. Nat. Hist. (7), i., 1898, pp 321 – 326.
† Mayr—Journ. Mus. Godeff., xii., 1876, p. 56 – 115.

Funafuti, has lately been re-taken at Fife Bay, British New Guinea.* The *Ceresium* occurs at Norfolk Island.

Hormurus australasiae, *Fabricius*.
Garypus longidigitatus, *Rainbow*.
Obisium antipodum, *Simon*.
Olpium longiventer, *Keyserling*.
Araneus theis, *var.* mangareva, *Walckenaer*.
    ,,   plebeja, *L. Koch*.
    ,,   ventricosa, *Rainbow*.
    ,,   longispina, *Rainbow*.
    ,,   etheridgei, *Rainbow*.
    ,,   festiva, *Rainbow*.
    ,,   obscura, *Rainbow*.
    ,,   annulipes, *Rainbow*.
    ,,   distincta, *Rainbow*.
    ,,   hoggi, *Rainbow*.
    ,,   speciosa, *Rainbow*.
Tetragnatha laqueata, *L. Koch*.
    ,,   panopea, *L. Koch*.
Uloborus geniculatus, *Olivieri*.
Dictis striatipes, *L. Koch*.
Clubiona alveolata, *L. Koch*.
Heteropoda venatoria, *Linne*.
Sarotes debilis, *L. Koch*.
Acompse suavis, *L. Koch*.
Ascyltus pterygodes, *L. Koch*.
Hyllus ferox, *Rainbow*.
    ,,   audax, *Rainbow*.
Oribata lamellata, *Rainbow*.

Class MYRIOPODA.

Scolopendra morsicans, *Linne*.
Otostigmus astenon, *Kohlrausch*.
Mecistocephalus punctifrons, *Newport*.
Orphmaeus phosphoreus, *Linne*.
Trichocambala sollasi, *Pocock*.

Class INSECTA.

Monocrepidius ferrugineus, *Montrouzier*.
    ,,   umbraculatus, *Candèze*.
Uloma cavicollis, *Fairm*.
    ,,   insularis, *Guérin*.
Sphenophorus sulcipes, *Karsch*.
    ,,   obscurus, *Boisduval*.
Elytrurus squamatus, *Rainbow*.
Nacerdes transmarina, *Rainbow*.

---

* Rainbow—Proc. Linn. Soc. N.S.W., xxiii., 1898, p. 365.

Ceresium simplex, *Gyllenhal.*
Concephalus ensiger, *Harold.*
Panesthia aethops, *Stoll.*
Loboptera decipiens, *Germain.*
Arachnocephalus vestitus, *Costa.*
Calotermes marginipennis, *Latreille.*
Megachile hedleyi, *Rainbow.*
Camponotus novœhollandiœ, *Mayr.*
Prenolepis vividula, *Nylander.*
Plagiolepis gracilis, *Smith.*
Meranoplus oceanicus, *Smith.*
     ,,   pubescens, *Smith.*
Pheidole sexspinosa, *Mayr.*
     ,,   oceanica, *Mayr.*
Euphloea eleutho, *Quoy and Gaimard.*
     ,,   distincta, *Butler.*
Junonia vellida, *Fabricius.*
Diadema nerina, *Fabricius.*
     ,,   otaheitœ, *Felder.*
Deiopea pulchella, *Linne.*
Achœa melicerto, *Drury.*
Remigia translata, *Walker.*
Chloanges suralis, *Zeller.*
Amyna octo, *Guènèe.*
Erilita modestalis, *Lederer.*
Rinecera mirabilis, *Butler.*
Harpagoneura complexa, *Butler.*
Halobates *sp.*
Culex hispiodosus, *Skuse.*
Megarrhina inornata, *Walker.*
Lispe vittata, *Rainbow.*
Degeeria dawsoni, *Rainbow.*
Ebenia nigricruris *Rainbow.*
     ,,   fieldi, *Rainbow.*

Class MOLLUSCA.

Loligo brevipinnis, *Pfeffer.*
Octopus tonganus, *Hoyle.*
Scissurella œquatoria, *Hedley.*
Schisomope plicata, *Hedley.*
Haliotis stomatiœformis, *Reeve.*
     ,,   ovina, *Chemnitz.*
Emarginula clathrata, *Pease.*
     ,,   mariei, *Crosse.*
Acmœa saccharina, *Linne.*
Phenacolepas senta, *Hedley.*
Trochus obeliscus, *Gmelin.*
     ,,   tubiferus, *Kiener.*
     ,,   atropurpureus, *Gould.*

Trochus fastigatus, *A. Adams.*
Gibbula concinna, *Dunker.*
    „   phasianella, *Deshayes.*
Monilea lifuana, *Fischer.*
    „   tragema, *Melvill and Standen.*
Euchelus instrictus, *Gould.*
Teinostoma qualum, *Hedley.*
    „   parvulum, *Hedley.*
    „   rotatum, *Hedley.*
    „   tricarinatum, *Melvill and Standen.*
Cirsonella ovata, *Hedley.*
Liotia crenata, *Kiener.*
    „   *sp.*
    „   *sp.*
    „   parvissima, *Hedley.*
Mecoliotia halligani, *Hedley.*
Phasianella wisemanni, *Baird.*
    „   minima, *Melvill.*
Stomatella sanguinea, *A. Adams.*
Stomatia phymotis, *Helbling.*
Gena rosacea, *Pease.*
Turbo petholatus, *var.* caledonicus, *Fischer.*
    „   setosus, *Gmelin.*
    „   argyrostomus, *Linne.*
Astralium petrosum, *Martyn.*
Leptothyra lacta, *Montrouzier.*
Delphinula lacinata, *Lamarck.*
Neritopsis radula, *Linne.*
Nerita albicilla, *Linne.*
    „   maxima, *Chemnitz.*
    „   plicata, *Linne.*
    „   polita, *Linne.*
    „   insculpta, *Recluz.*
Neritina reticulata, *Sowerby.*
Helicina musiva, *var.* rotundata, *Mousson.*
Eulima pyramidalis, *A. Adams.*
    „   samoensis, *Crosse.*
    „   diaphana, *Hedley.*
    „   decipiens, *Hedley.*
Stylifer varicifer, *Hedley.*
Odontostomia bulimoides, *Sowerbie.*
    „   rubra, *Pease.*
    „   robusta, *Hedley.*
    „   biplicata, *Hedley.*
Pyramidella dolabrata, *var.* terebelloides, *A. Adams.*
    „   turrita, *A. Adams.*
    „   mitralis, *A. Adams.*

Js

Obtortio pyrrhacme, *Melvill and Standen*.
Scala revoluta, *Hedley*.
„ paumotensis, *Pease*.
„ subauriculata, *Souverbie*.
„ ovalis, *Sowerby*.
Scaliola lapillifera, *Hedley*.
Ianthina *sp*.
Natica violacea, *Sowerby*.
„ marochiensis, *Gmelin*.
„ mamilla, *Linne*.
„ melanostoma, *Gmelin*.
„ umbilicata, *Quoy and Gaimard*.
Vanikoro gueriniana, *Recluz*.
Capulus intortus, *Lamarck*.
„ violaceus, *Angas*.
Hipponyx australis, *Quoy*.
Mitrularia equestris, *var.* tortilis, *Reeve*.
Truncatella valida, *Pfeiffer*.
Omphalotropis zebriolata, *Mousson*.
Assiminea nitida, *Pease*.
Rissoa invisibilis, *Hedley*.
„ finckhi, *Hedley*.
„ poolei, *Hedley*.
Rissoina exasperata, *Souverbie*.
„ gemmea, *Hedley*.
„ polytropa, *Hedley*.
„ plicata, *Adams*.
„ ambigua, *Gould*.
„ affinis, *Garrett*.
Diala virgata, *Hedley*.
„ hardyi, *Melvill and Standen*.
„ profunda, *Hedley*.
Solarium hybridum, *Linne*.
Heliacus discoideus, *Pease*.
Littorina obesa, *Sowerby*.
Modulus tectum, *Gmelin*.
Risella conoidalis, *Pease*.
Plesiotrochus souverbianus, *Fischer*.
Fossarus lamellosus, *Montrouzier*.
Planaxis sulcatus, *Born*.
„ lineatus, *Da Costa*.
Melania mageni, *Gassies*.
Caecum vertebrale, *Hedley*.
„ exile, *De Folin*.
„ gulosum, *Hedley*.
„ amaltheanum, *Hedley*.
„ legumen, *Hedley*.

Vermetus maximus, *Sowerby.*

„   *sp.*

Turritella concava, *Martens.*

Strombus lentiginosus, *Linne.*

„   floridus, *Lamarck.*

„   dentatus, *var.* rugosus, *Sowerby.*

„   hæmastoma, *Sowerby.*

„   terebellatus, *Sowerby.*

„   gibberulus, *Linne.*

„   samar, *Dillwyn.*

„   luhuanus, *Linne.*

Pterocera aurantia, *Lamarck.*

„   byronia, *Gmelin.*

„   rugosa, *Sowerby.*

Terebellum subulatum, *Lamarck.*

Cerithium nodulosum, *Bruguière.*

„   columna, *Sowerby.*

„   citrinum, *Sowerby.*

„   echinatum, *Lamarck.*

„   maculosum, *Mighels.*

„   rostratum, *Sowerby.*

„   oceanicum, *Hedley.*

„   breve, *var.* ellicense, *Hedley.*

„   spiculum, *Hedley.*

„   strictum, *Hedley.*

„   variegatum, *Quoy and Gaimard.*

„   zebrum, *Kiener.*

„   impendens, *Hedley.*

„   piperitum, *Sowerby.*

„   obeliscus, *Bruguière.*

„   „   *var.* cedo-nulli, *Sowerby.*

„   asperum, *Linne.*

„   pharos, *Hinds.*

„   elegantissimum, *Hedley.*

Contumax decollatus, *Hedley.*

Cerithiopsis eutrapela, *Melvill and Standen.*

„   electrina, *Hedley.*

Triforis dolicha, *Watson.*

„   aegle, *Jousseaume.*

„   torquatus, *Hedley.*

„   ruber, *Hinds.*

„   clio, *Hedley.*

„   obesula, *Jousseaume.*

„   thetis, *Hedley.*

„   incisus, *Pease.*

„   corrugatus, *Hinds.*

„   asperrimus, *Hinds.*

„   *spp.*

Ovula hervieri, *Hedley*.
Cypraea argus, *Linne*.
„ scurra, *Chemnitz*.
„ testudinaria, *Linne*.
„ isabella, *Linne*.
„ carneola, *Linne*.
„ „ *var.* propinqua, *Garrett*.
„ talpa, *Linne*.
„ goodalli, *Gray*.
„ fimbriata, *Gmelin*.
„ macula, *Adams*.
„ mauritiana, *Linne*.
„ caput-serpentis, *Linne*.
„ mappa, *Linne*.
„ arabica, *Linne*.
„ reticulata, *Martyn*.
„ moneta, *Linne*.
„ „ *var.* annulus, *Linne*.
„ tigris, *Linne*.
„ vitellus, *Linne*.
„ lynx, *Linne*.
„ clandestina, *var.* artuffeli, *Jousseaume*.
„ cribraria, *Linne*.
„ becki, *Gaskoin*.
„ erosa, *Linne*.
„ poraria, *Linne*.
„ helvola, *Linne*.
„ cicercula, *Linne*.
„ nucleus, *Linne*.
„ childreni, *Gray*.
Trivia oryza, *Lamarck*.
Dolium perdix, *Linne*.
„ pomum, *Linne*.
Cassis cornuta, *Linne*.
„ vibex, *var.* erinacea, *Linne*.
Tritonium tritonis, *Linne*.
„ pileare, *Linne*.
„ chlorostomum, *Lamarck*.
„ gemmatum, *Reeve*.
„ digitale, *Reeve*.
„ tuberosum, *Lamarck*.
„ maculosum, *Gmelin*.
Distortrix anus, *Linne*.
Gyrineum bufonium, *Gmelin*.
„ affine, *Broderip*.
Peristernia nassatula, *Lamarck*.
Latirus polygonus, *var.* barclayi, *Reeve*.
„ craticulatus, *Linne*.

Pisania fasciculata, *Reeve*.
Cantharus undosus, *Linne*.
Murex ramosus, *Linne*.
,, adustus, *Lamarck*.
,, funafutiensis, *Hedley*.
,, radula, *Hedley*.
Purpura hippocastaneum, *Lamarck*.
,, armigera, *Chemnitz*.
Jopas sertum, *Bruguière*.
Sistrum hystrix, *Linne*.
,, horridum, *Lamarck*.
,, ricinus, *Linne*.
,, morus, *Lamarck*.
,, digitatum, *Lamarck*.
,, tuberculatum, *Blainville*.
,, cancellatum, *Quoy*.
,, fiscellum, *Chemnitz*.
Coralliophila coronata, *Barclay*.
Galeropsis madreporarum, *Sowerby*.
Magilus antiquus, *Lamarck*.
Nassa semitexta. *Hedley*.
,, granifera, *Kiener*.
Columbella varians, *Sowerby*.
,, galaxias, *Reeve*.
,, melvilli, *Hedley*.
,, alofa, *Hedley*.
,, obtusa, *Sowerby*.
,, tringa, *Lamarck*.
,, rubicunda, *Quoy and Gaimard*.
Engina parva, *Pease*.
,, nodicostata, *Pease*.
,, mendicaria, *Linne*.
Mitra episcopalis, *Linne*.
,, pontificalis, *Lamarck*.
,, flammea *var*. hystrix, *Montrouzier*.
,, cucumerina, *Lamarck*.
,, chrysalis, *Reeve*.
,, tabanula *var*. caledonica, *Recluz*.
,, ferruginea, *Lamarck*.
,, acuminata. *Swainson*.
,, brunnea, *Pease*.
,, astricta, *Reeve*.
,, limbifera, *Lamarck*.
,, litterata, *Lamarck*.
,, paupercula, *Linne*.
,, virgata, *Reeve*.
Turricula gruneri, *Reeve*.
,, exasperata, *Chemnitz*.

Turricula angulosa, *Kuster.*
„ variata, *Reeve.*
„ nodosa, *Swainson.*
„ pilsbryi, *Hedley.*
Cylindra dactylus, *Linne.*
Erato schmeltziana, *Crosse.*
Marginella sandwicensis, *Pease.*
„ iota, *Hedley.*
„ peasii, *Reeve.*
„ isseli, *var.* ellicensis. *Hedley.*
Olivella simplex, *Pease.*
Oliva guttata, *Lamarck.*
„ irisans, *var.* erythrostoma, *Lamarck.*
Harpa minor, *Lamarck.*
„ gracilis, *Broderip and Sowerby.*
Drillia unizonalis, *Lamarck.*
Glyphostoma purpurascens, *Dunker.*
„ alicea, *Melvill and Standen.*
„ „ *var.* tenera, *Hedley.*
„ malleti, *Recluz.*
Thetidos morsura, *Hedley.*
Mangilia himerta, *Melvill and Standen.*
Clathurella lactea, *Reeve.*
„ clandestina, *Deshayes.*
„ apicalis, *Montrouzier.*
„ irretita, *Hedley.*
Daphnella delicata, *Reeve.*
„ lymneiformis, *Kiener.*
„ pupoidea, *H. Adams.*
„ thiasotes, *Melvill and Standen.*
Conus literatus, *Linne.*
„ tessellatus, *Born.*
„ pulicarius, *Hwass.*
„ hebraeus, *Linne*
„ „ *var.* vermiculatus, *Hwass.*
„ ceylonensis, *Hwass.*
„ vexillum, *Gmelin.*
„ rattus, *Hwass.*
„ capitaneus, *Linne.*
„ lividus, *Hwass.*
„ „ *var.* flavidus, *Lamarck.*
„ vitulinus, *Hwass.*
„ catus, *Hwass.*
„ nussatella, *Linne.*
„ striatus, *Linne.*
„ geographus, *Linne.*
„ tulipa, *Linne.*
„ auratus, *Linne.*

Terebra crenulata, *Linne.*
,, dimidiata, *Linne.*
,, maculata, *Linne.*
,, subulata, *Linne.*
,, tigrina, *Gmelin.*
,, affinis, *Gray.*
Pterosoma plana, *Lesson.*
Atlanta gibbosa, *Eydoux and Souleyet.*
,, turriculata, *D'Orbigny.*
,, guidichaudi, *Eydoux and Souleyet.*
Solidula sulcata, *Gmelin.*
Tornatina voluta, *Quoy and Gaimard.*
,, hadfieldi, *Melvill and Standen.*
,, leptekes, *Watson.*
Retusa waughiana, *Hedley.*
Atys cylindrica, *Hebling.*
,, hyalina, *Watson.*
,, dentifera, *A. Adams.*
,, dactylus, *Hedley.*
Cylichna erecta, *Hedley.*
Haminea vitrea, *A. Adams.*
Cylindrobulla sculpta, *Nevill.*
Akera aperta, *Hedley.*
Hydatina amplustre, *Linne.*
,, physis, *Linne.*
Ringicula parvula, *Hedley.*
,, incisa, *Hedley.*
,, *sp.*
Limacina inflata *D'Orbigny.*
,, bulimodes, *D'Orbigny.*
Clio virgula, *Rang.*
,, acicula, *Rang.*
,, striata, *Rang.*
,, subula, *Quoy and Gaimard.*
,, pyramidata, *Linne.*
Cuvierina columella, *Rang.*
Cavolinia quadridentata, *Lesueur.*
,, longirostris, *Lesueur.*
,, inflexa, *Lesueur.*
Agadina stimpsoni, *A. Adams.*
Elysia nigropunctata, *var.* sanguinea, *Hedley.*
Phyllidia varicosa, *Lamarck.*
Plecotrema bellum, *H. and A. Adams.*
,, mordax, *Dohrn.*
Melampus fasciatus, *Deshayes.*
,, luteus, *Quoy and Gaimard.*
Tornatellina oblonga, *Pease.*
,, conica, *Mousson.*

Vertigo pediculus, *Shuttleworth.*
Stenogyra gracilis, *Hutton.*
Endodonta modicella, *Ferussac.*
    ,,   decemplicata, *Mousson.*
Trochonanina samoensis, *Mousson.*
Dentalium lessoni, *Deshayes.*
Cadulus aratus, *Hedley.*
Anomia *sp.*
Arca zebra, *Swainson.*
    ,,   maculata, *Sowerby.*
    ,,   reticulata, *Gmelin.*
    ,,   velata, *Sowerby.*
    ,,   tenella, *Reeve.*
    ,,   congenita, *Smith.*
    ,,   pteroessa, *Smith.*
Limopsis davidi, *Hedley.*
Septifer excisus, *Wiegman.*
Modiola australis, *Gray.*
Lithophaga teres, *Philippi.*
    ,,   levigata, *Quoy and Gaimard.*
Plicatula imbricata, *Menke.*
Spondylus ocellatus, *Reeve.*
Lima bullata, *Sowerby.*
    ,,   tenera, *Chemnitz.*
    ,,   squamosa, *Lamarck.*
    ,,   angulata, *Sowerby.*
    ,,   fragilis, *Gmelin.*
Limea pectinata, *H. Adams.*
Pecten squamatus, *Gmelin.*
    ,,   pallium, *Linne.*
    ,,   distans, *Reeve.*
    ,,   madreporarum, *Sowerby.*
    ,,   speciosus, *Reeve.*
Hinnites *sp.*
Pteria peasei, *Dunker.*
    ,,   cumingii, *Reeve.*
Melina samoensis, *Baird.*
Pinna *sp.*
Ostrea hanleyana, *Sowerby.*
    ,,   cristagalli, *Linne.*
Cardita sweeti, *Hedley.*
Lucina exasperata, *Reeve.*
    ,,   punctata, *Linne.*
    ,,   divergens, *Philippi.*
    ,,   oblonga, *Hedley.*
Corbis fimbriata, *Linne.*
Cryptodon globosum, *Forskal.*
Tellina rugosa, *Born.*

Tellina scobinata, *Linne*.

",, flammula, *Deshayes*.

",, dispar, *Conrad*.

",, obliquaria, *Deshayes*.

",, rhomboides, *Quoy and Gaimard*.

",, robusta, *Hanley*.

",, opalina, *Sowerby*.

",, fijiensis, *Sowerby*.

",, crebrimaculata, *Sowerby*.

",, ellicensis, *Hedley*.

Libitina guinaica, *Lamarck*.

Circe pectinata, *Linne*.

",, picta, *Lamarck*.

",, castrensis, *Linne*.

Cytherea obliquata, *var*. prora, *Conrad*.

",, subpellucida, *Sowerby*.

Venus toreuma, *Gould*.

",, puerpera, *var*. listeri, *Gray*.

Venerupis macrophylla, *Deshayes*.

Naranio lapicida, *Chemnitz*.

Crassatella *sp*.

Kellya pacifica, *Hedley*.

Scintilla semiclausa, *Sowerby*.

Atactodea striata, *Gmelin*.

Asaphis deflorata, *Linne*.

Psammobia squammosa, *Lamarck*.

Cardium angulatum, *Lamarck*.

",, maculosum, *Wood*.

",, cardissa, *var*. dionæum, *Sowerby*.

",, fragrum, *Linne*.

",, ,, *var*. suezicnse, *Issel*.

Tridacna gigas, *var*. squamosa, *Lamarck*.

",, elongata, *Lamarck*.

Chama imbricata, *Broderip*.

",, spinosa, *Broderip*.

",, unicornis, *Bruguière*.

Corbula tahcitensis, *Lamarck*.

Gastrochæna lamellosa, *Deshayes*.

Nausitoria aurita, *Hedley*.

Tonicia *sp*.

Class BRACHIOPODA.

Thecidea maxilla, *Hedley*.

Class ECHINODERMATA.

To the Echinodermata enumerated in the body of this work there are added in the following list the species collected by

J. S. Gardiner, and determined by F. P. Bedford and F. J. Bell.*
A sea-urchin, believed to be *Metalia sternalis*, Gray, was occasionally found dead at high-water mark on the beaches of the
leeward islets of Funafuti, but as no specimens were preserved for
exact identification, it is not here included. A starfish dredged
off the north-west corner of Funafuti, at a depth of one hundred
and thirty fathoms by H.M.S. "Penguin," which was, in life,
bordered by segments of brick-red and yellow-red, size R. 30 mm.,
has been presented to the Australian Museum by Lieutenant A.
Waugh, R.N. This has been determined by Mr. Whitelegge as
probably an immature example of *Nardoa gomophia*, Perrier,
originally described from New Caledonia.†

Echinothrix diadema, *Linne*.
,, turcarum, *Schynvoet*.
Heterocentrotus mamillatus, *Klein*.
Echinometra lucunter, *Leske*.
,, oblonga, *Blainville*.
Echinus angulosus, *Leske*.
Laganum depressum, *Lesson*.
Echinoneus cyclostomus, *Leske*.
Maretia planulata. *Lamarck*.
Ophidiaster cylindricus, *Lamarck*.
Linckia pacifica, *Gray*.
Nardoa gomophia, *Perrier*.
Culcita acutispina, *Bell*.
Ophiactis savignii, *Muller and Troschel*.
Ophiocoma scolopendrina, *Agassiz*.
,, erinaceus, *Muller and Troschel*.
Ophiarthrum elegans, *Peters*.
Mulleria echinites, *Jaeger*.
,, parvula, *Selenka*.
Holothuria argus, *Jaeger*.
,, atra, *Jaeger*.
,, ,, var. amboinensis, *Semper*.
,, vagabunda, *Selenka*.
., maculata, *Brandt*.
,, imitans, *Ludwig*.
Chiridota intermedia, *Bedford*.
Synapta ooplax, *Marenzeller*.

Class ANNELIDA.

Eurythoe complanata, *Pallas*.
,, pacifica, var. levukænsis, *McIntosh*.
Phyllodoce *sp*.
Perichæta grubei, *Rosa*.
,, *sp*.

* Bedford and Bell—Proc. Zool. Soc., 1898, pp. 834–850.
† Perrier—Archiv. Zool. Exper., iv., 1875, p. 431.

Class GEPHYREA.

To the list of Gephyrean worms recorded by A. E. Shipley from Funafuti,* has been added *A. steenstrupii*, identified (*ante* p. 394) by Mr. Whitelegge. The distribution of most of these has been further elucidated by Shipley in a Report on the Willey Collection.†

Sipunculus vastatus, *Selenka and Bulow.*
,, funafuti, *Shipley.*
Physcosoma nigrescens, *Keferstein.*
,, pacificum. *Keferstein.*
,, scolops, *Selenka and de Man.*
,, varians, *Keferstein.*
,, microdontodon, *Sluiter.*
,, dentigerum, *Selenka and de Man.*
Aspidosiphon elegans, *Chamisso and Eysenhardt.*
,, steenstrupii, *Diesing.*
,, klunzingeri, *Selenka and Bulow.*
Cloeosiphon aspergillum, *Quatrefages.*

Class PORIFERA.

Reuiera australis, *Lendenfeld.*
,, *sp.*
Halichondria solida *var.* rugosa, *Ridley and Dendy.*
Spinosella glomerata, *Whitelegge.*
Gellius aculeatus, *Whitelegge.*
Clathria pellicula, *Whitelegge.*
Agelas gracilis, *Whitelegge.*
Echinodictyum asperum, *Ridley and Dendy.*
Acanthella stipitata, *Carter.*
,, pulcherrima, *Ridley and Dendy.*
Ciocalypta incrustans. *Whitelegge.*
Polymastia dendyi, *Whitelegge.*
Spirastrella papillosa. *Ridley and Dendy.*
Euspongia irregularis *var.* silicata, *Lendenfeld.*
Hippospongia dura, *Lendenfeld.*
Spongelia fragilis *var.* irregularis, *Lendenfeld.*

Class HYDROZOA.

A dead specimen of *Distichopora rosea* was collected on the beach but was overlooked in packing. Some notes on *Millepora* from Funafuti have been published by Prof. S. J. Hickson.‡

Thuiaria divergens, *Whitelegge.*
Aglaophenia clavicula, *Whitelegge.*
Millepora squarrosa, *Lamarck.*
,, platyphylla, *Ehrenberg.*

* Shipley—Proc. Zool. Soc., 1898, pp. 468–473.
† Willey—Zoological Results, part 2, 1899, p. 151–158.
‡ Hickson—Proc. Zool. Soc., 1898, p. 828.

Millepora nodosa, *Esper*.
     ,,   tortuosa, *Dana*.
Distichopora rosea, *Kent*.
Physalia megalista, *Lamarck*.

Class SCYPHOZOA.

Aurelia clausa, *Lesson*.
Polyrhiza orithyia, *Haeckel*.

Class ACTINOZOA.

The following list of Actinozoa is compiled from different sources under the supervision of Mr. Whitelegge, whose papers in this volume (pp. 213 – 225, 307 – 320, 349 – 368, and 384 – 391) have formed the basis. With these have been incorporated information from the articles of J. S. Gardiner and I. L. Hiles.*

In some prefatory notes to the Mollusca, it was remarked that the high proportion of novelties to the mass of previously known forms should not be mistaken for an indication of endemic importance, but should be ascribed to the imperfection of our knowledge of the continental faunas. This statement has received support from the Gorgonidæ in the brief time that has elapsed since it was written. *Keroeides gracilis* has been retaken by Willey in New Guinea, *Villogorgia rubra* by Willey in the Loyalty Islands, *Acamptogogia spinosa* by Willey in New Britain, *Lobophytum hedleyi* and *L. densum* by Hedley in New Caledonia.

Some giant specimens of a white Sea Anemone, ten inches in diameter, were observed on Funafuti, but defied any effort to remove them and are hence unnoted in the following list.

The specific identification of Reef Corals is regarded by the highest authorities as a matter of extreme uncertainty. H. M. Bernard wrote :—" The only specimens which can be claimed with absolute certainty as specifically identical are a few which have in each case been gathered at the same place and time, and resemble one another as closely as if they were two fragments of one and the same stock. Beyond these no certainty exists, and strict regard to the variations of form and structure would compel us to label all the remaining specimens as different varieties or species."†
To maintain such a position means chaos. Either we must, as Bernard proceeds to suggest, " break loose from the restraint of the Linnean species," or deal with the group on the broader lines on which Hickson has lately dealt with the *Heliopora* and *Millepora*.

---

* Gardiner—Proc. Zool. Soc., 1897, pp. 941 – 953; Idem 1898, pp. 257 – 276, 525 – 539, and 994 – 1000; Hiles, in Willey, Zoological Results, part 2, 1899, pp. 193 – 204.

† Bernard—Cat. Madreporarian Corals Brit. Mus.. 1896, p. 20.

Finding ourselves unable to reconcile the species enumerated by Whitelegge and Gardiner the results arrived at by each are given in parallel columns.

Sarcophytum glaucum, *Quoy and Gaimard.*
,, trochoheliophorum *var.* amboinense, *Marenzeller.*
,, latum, *Dana.*
Lobophytum pauciflorum *var.* validum, *Marenzeller.*
,, hedleyi, *Whitelegge.*
,, marenzelleri, *Wright and Studer.*
,, tuberculosum, *Quoy and Gaimard.*
,, confertum, *Dana.*
,, densum, *Whitelegge.*
,, viride, *Quoy and Gaimard.*
Spongodes pallida. *Whitelegge*
,, curvicornis, *Wright and Studer.*
Siphonogorgia godeffroyi, *Kölliker.*
,, pallida, *Studer.*
,, kollikeri, *Wright and Studer.*
,, macrospina, *Whitelegge.*
Heliopora caerulea, *Pallas.*
Keroides gracilis, *Whitelegge.*
Acamptogorgia spinosa, *Hiles.*
Acanthogorgia breviflora, *Whitelegge.*
Acanthomuricea simplex, *Whitelegge.*
Villogorgia flagellata, *Whitelegge.*
,, intricata, *Gray.*
,, ruber, *Hiles.*
Bebryce studeri, *Whitelegge.*
Muricella purpurea, *Whitelegge.*
Plexaura antipathes, *Esper.*
Nicella laxa, *Whitelegge.*
Verrucella flabellata, *Whitelegge.*
Antipathella brookii, *Whitelegge.*
Zoanthus funafutiensis, *Hill and Whitelegge.*
Gemmaria willeyi, *Hill and Whitelegge.*
Palythoa howesi, *Haddon and Shackleton.*
,, kochii, *Haddon and Shackleton.*
,, coesia, *Dana.*

REEF CORALS

Reported from Funafuti by,—

Whitelegge.	*Gardiner.*
Caryophylla clavus *var.* epitheata, *Duncan.*	Rhizotrochus, *sp.*
Stylophora digitata, *Pallas.*	Stylophora digitata, *Pallas.*
	,, flabellata, *Quelch.*
	,, compressa, *Gardiner.*
	,, rugosa, *Gardiner.*

Whitelegge.

Gardiner.

Stylophora pistillata, *Esper.*
,, palmata, *Blainville.*
,, lobata, *Gardiner.*

Pocillopora grandis, *Dana.*
,, caespitosa, *Dana.*
,, 'verrucosa, *E. & Sol.*

Pocillopora, grandis, *Dana.*
,, glomerata, *Gardiner.*
,, rugosa, *Gardiner.*
,, mœandrina, *Dana.*
,, squarrosa, *Dana.*
,, aspera, *Verrill.*
,, ,, rar. danœ, *V.*
,, ,, rar. ligulata, *Dana.*
,, favosa, *Ehrenberg.*
,, clavaria, *Ehrenberg.*
,, brevicornis, *Lam.*
,, septata, *Gardiner.*
,, suffruticosa, *Verrill.*
,, paucistella, *Quelch.*
Seriatopora conferta, *Quelch.*
,, spinosa, *Ed. & Haime.*

Mussa costata, *Dana.*
Coeloria esperi, *Edw. and H.*
Hydnophora microconia, *Lam.*
Astræa versipora, *Dana.*
,, danœ, *Edw. and H.*
,, denticulata, *E. and Sol.*
Acanthastræa patula, *Dana.*
,, echinata, *Dana.*
Leptastræa solida, *Edw. and H.*
,, transversa, *Klunz.*
Cyphastræa danœ, *Edw. and H.*
Pavonia repens, *Bruggeman.*
,, explanata, *Lamarck.*
Psammocera contigua, *Esp.*
,, fossata, *Dana.*

Pavonia repens, *Bruggeman.*

Psammocera contigua, *Esp.*
,, haimeana, *Ed. & H.*
,, superficialis, *Gard.*
,, savigniensis, *Gard.*

Oxypora *sp.*
Fungia tenuidens, *Quelch.*
,, discus, *Dana.*

Halomitra irregularis, *Gardiner.*
Herpolitha crassa, *Gardiner.*

Madreporaria fruticosa, *Brook.*
,, syringodes, *Brook.*
,, spicifera, *Dana.*
,, botryodes, *Brook.*
rar. funafutiensis, *Whitelegge.*

Madreporaria fruticosa, *Brook.*
,, crateriformis, *Gardiner.*
,, secunda, *Dana.*
,, scabrosa, *Quelch.*
,, reticulata, *Brook.*

Whitelegge.

Madreporaria patula, *Brook.*
,, efflorescens, *Dana.*
,, eurystoma, *Klunz.*
,, spinulifera,
 Whitelegge.
,, impressa, *Whitelegge.*

Astræopora incrustans, *Bernard.*
,, ocellata, *Bernard.*
,, hirsuta, *Bernard*
Montipora verrucosa, *Dana.*
,, foveolata, *Dana.*
,, tuberosa, *Klunzinger.*
,, scabricula, *Dana.*
,, exserta, *Quelch.*

Porites lutea, *Edw. and H.*
,, lichen, *Dana.*
,, lobata, *Dana.*
,, crassa, *Quelch.*
,, mirabilis, *Quelch.*
,, gaimardi, *Edw. and H.*

Gardiner.

Madreporaria profunda. *Gard.*
,, surculosa, *Dana.*
,, latistella, *Brook.*
,, sinensis, *Brook.*
,, cuneata, *Dana.*
,, bœodáctyla, *Brook.*
,, loripes, *Brook.*
,, angulata, *Quelch.*

Astræopora listeri, *Bernard.*
,, tabulata, *Gardiner.*
,, ovalis, *Bernard.*
Montipora verrucosa, *Lamarck.*
,, profunda, *Bernard.*
,, caliculata. *Dana, var.*
 piriformis, *Bernard.*
,, saxea, *Bernard.*
,, incognita, *Bernard.*
,, granifera, *Bernard.*

Porites arenosa, *Esper.*
,, ,, *var.* lutea, *E.&H.*
,, ,, *var.* parvicellata,
 Gardiner.
,, purpurea, *Gardiner.*
,, trimurata, *Gardiner.*
,, umbellifera, *Gardiner.*
,, superfusa, *Gardiner.*
,, exilis, *Gardiner.*

Class FORAMINIFERA.

Pressure of Museum duties has unfortunately not allowed the preparation of a Report on the Foraminifera collected at Funafuti.

THE MOLLUSCA OF FUNAFUTI.

(SUPPLEMENT.)

By Charles Hedley,

Conchologist, Australian Museum.

In the year 1897, a second, and in 1898, a third expedition visited the Atoll of Funafuti in prosecution of the attempt to carry a bore through the coral formation. The mollusca herein described were obtained by these parties, chiefly by deep dredging, and were remitted to the Australian Museum by the Local Funafuti Committee of the Royal Society. This material reached the Writer too late for incorporation in the body of this Memoir. The results of a study of it are accordingly presented in this appendix.

This material is of importance since it illustrates a side of the Funafuti zoology which I had little opportunity of investigating personally, viz., that of the deeper water. Dredgings carried out by Mr. G. H. Halligan in one hundred and fifty fathoms, and again in two hundred fathoms, produced results of especial interest. In the latter depth he discovered a bed of the typical "Pteropod Ooze." The sample of his dredgings submitted to me, might have stood for the portrait of that deposit figured by Murray and Renard.*

This ooze has been chiefly studied in the Atlantic, and though its equal distribution in the Pacific is a matter of course, the present record is an interesting extension of the known range.

But the chief claim that this deposit has on our attention is that it appears in water of less depth than in any instance known heretofore. The least depth in which the "Challenger" obtained Pteropod Ooze was in 390 fathoms, the greatest 1,525 fathoms, the average being 1,044 fathoms.†

The following species already noted as from surface waters again occurred in greater depths:

Teinostoma tricarinatum—150 fathoms off Beacon Islet (Funamanu), and 36 fathoms north of Pava Islet.

Cisonella ovata—150 fathoms off Beacon Islet (Funamanu).

Stomatella sanguinea—36 fathoms N. 30° West of Pava, 45 – 52 fathoms off Tutaga Islet.

---

*Murray and Renard—Chall. Rep., Deep Sea Deposits, 1891, pl. xi. fig. 6.
† Murray and Renard—*loc. cit.*, p. 225.

Cæcum vertebrale—off Tutaga in 45 – 52, 50 – 60, and 200 fathoms; off Beacon Islet (Funamanu), at 150; and in 36 fathoms north; and 36 fathoms N. 30° W. of Pava. This is evidently from its abundance a native of the deeper water. Some of the examples from 150 and 200 fathoms have a few brown blotches on the shell.

Cæcum gulosum—dredged at every station with *C. vertebrale.*

Columbella varians—36 fathoms N. 30° W. of Pava.

Marginella iota—36 fathoms N. 30° W. of Pava, off Beacon Islet (Funamanu) in 150, and off Tutaga in 45 – 52 and 200 fathoms.

Marginella sandwicensis—150 fathoms off Beacon Islet (Funamanu).

Olivella simplex—36 fathoms N. of Pava.

Those species which are either new to science or have not been yet recorded from Funafuti are as under.

CEPHALOPODA.

OCTOPUS TONGANUS, *Hoyle.*

Hoyle, Chall. Rep., Zool., xvi., 1886, p. 83, pl. viii., figs. 1, 2.

One male specimen was procured in the lagoon by Mr. A. E. Finckh. The species has only been found before at Tonga.

POLYPLACOPHERA.

TONICIA *sp.*

(Fig. 59.)

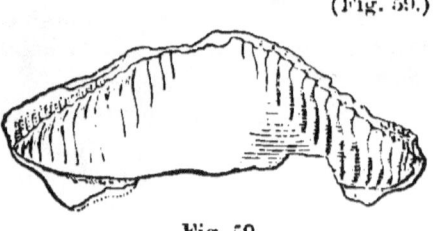

Fig. 59.

A single mutilated median valve of a Chiton was obtained at a depth of 150 fathoms off Beacon Islet (Funamanu). Such features as it has, point to an affinity with *T. confossa*, Gould. The rarity of this group in the Central Pacific renders the occurrence of this fragment noteworthy. Only six species were known to Harper Pease from the Central Pacific. In his last paper he stated that,—" The absence of Chitonidæ from Polynesia has been noticed by authors as a remarkable fact, abounding as they do* in the surrounding provinces, especially on the west coast of America, at Australia and New Zealand."†

---

* The Chitons not the authors.
† Pease—Am. Journ. Conch., vii., 1872, p. 194.

SCAPHOPODA.

CADULUS ARATUS, *sp. nov.*
(Fig. 60.)

Shell short and stout, slightly swollen and gently tapering to either end, on one side almost straight, on the other arcuate, glossy and almost transparent. In one case the translucent ground is mottled with opaque white spots. Four longitudinal equally spaced furrows impress the surface. Anal end bilabiate, the lips usually widely parted, that on the straighter side projecting beyond its fellow. In one case the lips are of equal length almost touching distally and divided by a narrow slit. Aperture very oblique with a small thickened rim. Length 3·4; breadth ·64 mm. Another specimen, length 2; breadth ·48 mm.

Dredged 36 fathoms north of Pava Islet; 36 fathoms N. 30° W. of Pava Islet; 50 – 60 fathoms off Tutaga Islet and 150 fathoms off Beacon Islet (Funamanu).

Fig. 60.

The Fijian *C. dichelus*, Watson, a near relative, is twice as large, more bent and unfurrowed.

GASTEROPODA.

SCISSURELLA EQUATORIA, *sp. nov.*
(Fig. 61.)

Shell large for the genus, thin, trochiform, with gradate spire; frilled, projecting keels; compressed belt below the fasciole, and tumid base. Colour white. Whorls five. Sculpture—about eighty five, curved, oblique, lamellate ribs cross the whole shell Above, the spiral sculpture can hardly be traced, but on the base it is distinguishable as delicate, widely spaced threads overriding the ribs and latticing the interspaces. Fasciole enfolded by broad margins, which are fimbriated by the ribs. Umbilicus narrow, infundibuliform, deep. Aperture oblique, subquadrate; lip slightly and gently recurved; columella margin explanate and reaching over the umbilicus. Major diameter 3, minor 2·5; height 2·68 m.m.

One specimen dredged off Tutaga Islet in 200 fathoms.

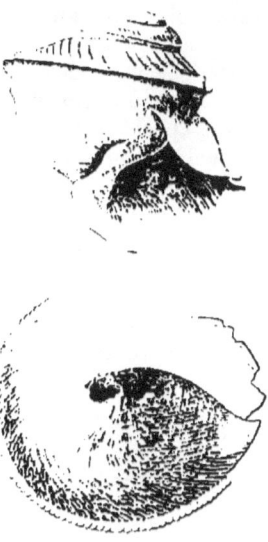

Fig 61

This, the largest species of the genus, seems very close to *S. iiedonia*, Watson, from which I separate it by the contracted zone beneath the fasciole, larger size and less development of spiral sculpture.

Schismope plicata, *sp. nov.*

(Fig. 62.)

Fig. 62.

Shell large for the genus, thin, subglobose, flattened above. Colour cream. Whorls three, rapidly increasing. Earlier whorls wound in the same plane, the last steeply descending, sharply angled at the fasciole, compressed and then inflated beneath it. Umbilicus moderate in width, deep, with smooth walls. Sculpture—both above and below the fasciole the shell is ornamented by about twenty-two prominent longitudinal ribs, which project most beneath the fasciole half a whorl behind the mouth, from thence on they diminish considerably. These are overridden by close, sharp, raised, spiral lines, which cross the interstices and denticulate the crests of the ribs. Slit pointed anteriorly, rounded posteriorly, in length about a sixth of the circumference of the shell. The fasciole, a broad gutter with raised margins, its trough septate by continuations of the longitudinal ribs, ascends the spire for a whorl and a half, as in other Pacific species. Aperture ovate, columella slightly reflected. Major diameter 2·3, minor 1·7; height 2 mm.

Dredged off Beacon Islet (Funamanu), in 150 fathoms, and off Tutaga in 150 and 50 – 60 fathoms.

This species stands nearest to *S. ferriezi*, Crosse, from which it is clearly distinguished by a more elevated spire, coarser sculpture and larger size.

Teinostoma qualum, *var.* Paucicostatum, *var. nov.*

(Fig. 63.)

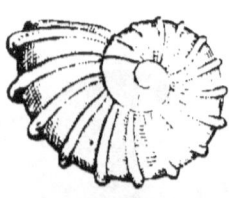

Fig. 63.

Under this varietal name is distinguished a specimen, which, though probably immature is larger than the type, measuring in major diameter 2 and in minor 1·32 mm. It has the same detail sculpture but carries sixteen ribs on the last whorl instead of twenty. The chief distinction however is that the ribs are continued to the suture instead of terminating at a distance therefrom as in the type.

Dredged at 150 fathoms off Beacon Islet (Funamanu).

HALIOTIS OVINA, *Chemnitz.*

Pilsbry, Man. Conch., xii., 1890, p. 125, pl. xix., figs. 7, 8.

A specimen was obtained at Funafuti by Mr. A. E. Finckh.

TEINOSTOMA PARVULUM, *sp. nov.*
(Fig. 64.)

Shell minute, solid, depressed turbinate, with slightly elevated spire. Colour cream. Whorls four. Sculpture—about fourteen elevated, spiral lyræ which are weaker and widest apart above and closer and stronger towards the umbilicus. Above and on the periphery, their interstices are occupied by one or two fine spiral threads. No transverse sculpture is apparent. Base rounded. Umbilicus oblong, narrow, deep; the basal sculpture winding obliquely into

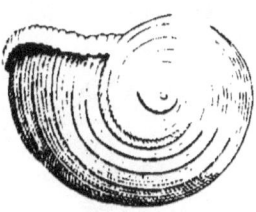

Fig. 64.

it. Aperture oblique, circular, with a smooth, inner, raised margin and a stout varix alternately and evenly grooved and ridged by the spiral sculpture. The left lower margin of the varix is produced in a tongue over the umbilicus. Major diameter 1·14, minor 1; height ·8 mm.

One specimen dredged in 36 fathoms north of Pava Islet.

This species, the least of the genus to which I have assigned it, has an equal claim to be placed in *Liotia.* The subumbilical tongue, a rather artificial feature, has governed the present generic disposition.

TEINOSTOMA ROTATUM, *sp. nov.*
(Fig. 65.)

Shell small, perforate, subdiscoidal. Colour white. Whorls three and a half, rounded, gradually increasing, last descending

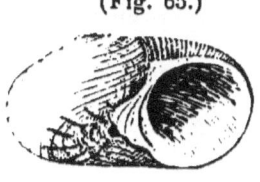
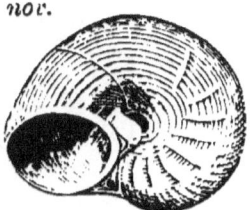

Fig. 65.

and contracting at the aperture. First two whorls smooth, the rest sculptured by about forty, fine, close, even, flat-topped, spiral lyræ; parted by sharp, narrow interstices. On the base are eight, raised, radiating bars of callus, unevenly set round the umbilicus, like the spokes of a wheel. A fifth of a whorl behind the aperture the scar of a former aperture has left a kind of varix. Umbilicus small, its margin crenulate. Aperture oblique, circular, entire; left margin barely recurved; lower right margin advancing over the umbilicus in imbricating callous tongues; upper right margin linked to the preceding whorl by a V-shaped callous ridge. Major diameter 1·86, minor 1·76; height 1·16 mm.

One specimen dredged in 200 fathoms off Tutaga Islet.

By its small size and peculiarly sculptured base, this species is sufficiently distinguished from the remainder of the genus.

Liotia *sp.*

(Fig. 66.)

Fig. 66.

Shell globose, rather flattened on the base. Colour cream. Whorls three. Sculpture—eight equally spaced spiral lyræ, cancellated by the intersection of about eighteen longitudinal ribs of equal size. Umbilicus narrow. Aperture unfinished. Major diameter 1·16, minor 1·6; height 1·16 mm.

One specimen in 200 fathoms off Tutaga Islet.

This shell, though not adult, is evidently new. Its future recognition should be ensured by the remarkable sculpture. Probably it belongs near *Liotia* and possibly to the new genus *Mecoliotia*. Until the important characters of the aperture are known, no good end would be served by bestowing on it a specific name.

Liotia parvissima, *sp. nov.*

(Fig. 67.)

Fig. 67.

Shell minute, solid, turbinate. Colour cream. Whorls four. Sculpture—a heavy, elevated keel on the shoulder, two equally massive on the periphery, and two smaller on the base. Across keels and interstices run distant, longitudinal, raised threads. Umbilicus small, oblique narrow and deep. Aperture, circular, oblique, with a short but heavy varix, crenulated by the spiral sculpture. Major diameter ·84, minor ·66; height ·84 mm.

Dredged off Tutaga Islet at a depth of 200 fathoms, and off Beacon Islet (Funamanu) at 150 fathoms.

This, the smallest known *Liotia*, is well distinguished by its simple and massive sculpture.

MECOLIOTIA, *gen. nov.*

A genus of the Liotiidæ, distinguished from *Liotia* by an elevated spire of six whorls, an obliquely truncate base and granose sculpture.

The type species appears to me to be co-generic with *Iphitus tuberculatus*, Watson.[*] The genus *Iphitus* was founded by Jeffreys on a single immature specimen,[†] and is known from Watson's rather than from Jeffreys' account. Jeffreys placed the genus in the Littorinidæ and Fisher in the Fossaridæ. My species cannot enter either of these families, nor, I should think, could *I. tuberculatus*. We are however, relieved from the unsatisfactory genus of Jeffreys by the fact that *Iphitus* is preoccupied in Mollusca by Rafinesque.[‡] In Hemiptera Stäl introduced *Iphita* in 1870.[§]

Type, *Mecoliotia halligani.*

MECOLIOTIA HALLIGANI, *sp. nov.*

(Fig. 68.)

Shell small, most massive, conical, with obliquely truncate base, narrowly perforate. Colour white. Whorls six of which two are apical, separated by deeply impressed sutures. Sculpture— the third has one, the fourth and fifth each two, and the last whorl three, prominent, heavy, spiral keels. These are overridden and knotted by longitudinal ribs, which on the last whorl number seventeen, cross from umbilicus to suture, and mount the upper whorls perpendicularly and continuously. Deep square pits are enclosed by the inter-

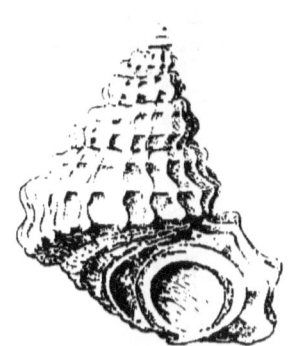

Fig. 68.

section of this sculpture. The first whorl is rounded, the second keeled. The base is hollow beneath the periphery, with a central

---

[*] Watson—Chall. Rep., Zool., xv., 1886, p. 583, pl. xlvi., fig. 5.

[†] Jeffreys—Proc. Zool. Soc., 1883, p. 113, pl. xx., fig. 12.

[‡] Rafinesque—Anal. Nat., 1815, p. 141.

[§] Stäl—Sv. Ak. Handl., 1870, p. 99.

nodose lyra, then a furrow, followed by the smooth raised margin of the narrow oblique umbilicus. Aperture, oblique, circular with a double lip, one within the other, and an expanded, trifid wing-like varix. Length 1·6; breadth 1·4 mm.

One specimen dredged off Tutaga Islet in 50 – 60 fathoms.

Named in honour of Mr. G. H. Halligan, who procured most of the deeper water species mentioned in this supplement.

EULIMA DIAPHANA, *sp. nov.*

(Fig. 69.)

Shell narrow, subulate, transparent. Whorls seven, rapidly increasing, wound more obliquely as the growth proceeds. Surface smooth, most glossy, through it is seen every detail of the columella. Aperture somewhat claw-shaped, narrow and curved, acuminate posteriorly, broadest and truncate anteriorly. Outer lip sharp sinuous. Columella slightly curved, spreading a callus on the preceding whorl. Length 1·8; breadth ·44 mm.

One specimen dredged at 45 – 52 fathoms off Tutaga.

This species appears to be widely different from any hitherto figured.

Fig. 69.

EULIMA SAMOENSIS, *Crosse.*

Tryon, Man. Conch., viii., 1886, pl. lxx., fig. 78.

One specimen collected by Mr. W. Poole on the lagoon beach was by him presented to the Australian Museum. The species was previously only known from Samoa.

ODONTOSTOMIA ROBUSTA, *sp. nov.*

(Fig. 70.)

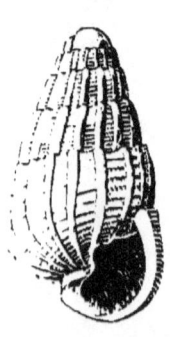

Shell small, strong, ovate. Colour white. Whorls four ; exclusive of the smooth, prostrate, heterostrophic two-whorled apex. Sculpture— sixteen strong, smooth, outstanding, longitudinal ribs sinuate the suture and reach to the extreme point of the base. Similar ribs extend continuously across the upper whorls. Between these ribs appear the broken lengths of about a dozen, delicate, widely parted, raised, spiral threads. Aperture ear-shaped, effuse anteriorly. Columella massive, entering in a strong, spiral twist. Lip formed by the last rib. Length 1·2; breadth ·65 mm.

Fig. 70.

One specimen dredged off Tutaga Islet in 45 – 52 fathoms.

This species is most like *O. oodes*, Watson, from which it is separated by more conical shape, fewer ribs and different apex.

ODONTOSTOMIA BIPLICATA, *sp. nov.*

(Fig 71.)

Shell oblong-ovate, imperforate, white. Whorls three and an inrolled vertical and half buried apex, slightly gradate, separated by a channeled suture. Upper whorls angled and contracted above the suture. Last whorl slightly angled at the periphery. Sculpture—last whorl with two small, but sharp revolving ridges, one at the periphery and the other below the suture, both ascending the earlier whorls. Upper whorls otherwise smooth, final whorl furrowed spirally by about twenty-five fine close grooves beneath the periphery. Aperture ovate, acuminate above and below. Deep within the throat and confined to the posterior moiety, are five strong revolving ridges, the remainder of the throat is grooved

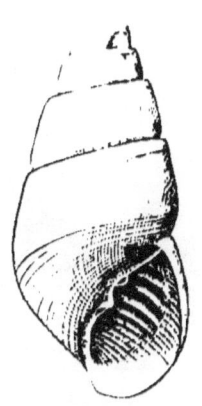

Fig. 71.

by small revolving striæ, answering to the externals culpture. Lip sharp, simple, produced anteriorly. Columella with a heavy, median, transverse fold, posterior to which is another deeper oblique fold. Length 1·46; breadth ·7 mm.

One specimen dredged at 36 fathoms north of Pava Islet.

This is a well marked species. Not only is it smaller than any enumerated in Tryon's Monograph, but the second, deep seated columella fold seems to be unmatched in the genus. The ridges in the throat occur in some species from the Red Sea.

RISSOA FINCKHII, *sp. nov.*
(Fig. 72.)

Shell narrow, subulate, turretted, massive, small. Colour white with a yellow apex. Whorls eight. Sculpture–round the periphery of each whorl is wound a heavy tabulate keel. The penultimate whorl carries a spiral thread above and another below this keel. On the last whorl is a raised subsutural thread and three basal lyræ. Aperture oblique, circular, peristome entire, thickened and broadly reflected. Length 1·92; breadth ·92 mm.

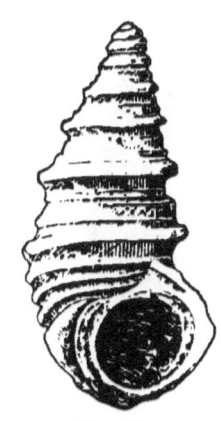

One specimen dredged off Tutaga Islet in 200 fathoms.

Named in honour of Mr. A. E. Finckh, who made zoological collections on Funafuti

Fig. 72.

in 1898, when in charge of the Diamond Drill Boring
Expedition.

Rissoa poolei, *sp. nov.*

(Fig. 73.)

Shell broadly ovate. Whorls four.
Colour white with a few subsutural orange
dots, one of which occurs on the lip and
three on the remainder of the last whorl.
Sculpture—the last whorl is angled at a
weak spiral rib on the periphery. Proportionately stronger are three on the
penultimate, and two on the antipenultimate, similar spiral ribs. The whole shell
is closely covered by minute, close, wavy,
spiral threads which are overridden by
faint, close, longitudinal sculpture extending across the whole whorl. Umbilicus
small, covered by the columella. Aperture
round, rather oblique. Lip massive, expanded and broadly
reflected with a second lip or varix close behind. Columella
broad appressed. Length ·95; breadth ·66 mm.

Fig. 73.

Dredged off Tutaga Islet at depths of 45 – 52, 50 – 60, and 200
fathoms; off Beacon Islet (Funamanu) at 150 fathoms; and north
of Pava Islet at 36 fathoms.

The affinities of this shell are with the species previously
described from Funafuti as *Rissoa invisibilis.* It is named in
honour of Mr. William Poole, B.A., a volunteer assistant of the
second expedition to Funafuti.

Diala profunda, *sp. nov.*

(Fig. 74.)

Shell subulate, thin. Colour, the figured example
has the first four whorls ochraceous, the next two
almost white, the last two ochraceous buff with the
columella and lip tawny; another specimen is uniform dark brown. Whorls eight. The apex smooth
and blunt; the third and fourth whorls with two
raised spiral cords each, the remaining whorls
angled above and below the suture. Surface
smooth and shining. Aperture perpendicular,
angled above, rounded below; outer lip straight
and sharp; columella reflected over a minute perforation. Length 1·9; breadth ·66 mm.

Fig. 74.

Dredged off Tutaga Islet at depths of 45 – 50,
50 – 60 and 200 fathoms; and in 36 fathoms north
and 36 fathoms N. 30° W. of Pava Islet.

CÆCUM AMALTHEANUM, *sp. nov.*
(Fig. 75.)

Shell small, a twisted cone, performing about a third of a revolution, rapidly enlarging. White very glossy, with about twenty, faint rib rings. Aperture circular, slightly contracted behind the everted lip. Septum gradate, with three steps, arising deep within the collar, peaked on the outer side. Length ·76; breadth at aperture ·34 mm.

Fig. 75.

Two examples dredged at 36 fathoms, north of Pava Islet.

The contour of this species isolates it from any co-generic type.

CÆCUM LEGUMEN, *sp. nov.*
(Fig. 76.)

Shell pod-shaped, arched on one side, nearly straight on the other; rounded in transverse section on the arched side and flattened on the straight. Colour white. Sculptured by fine growth rings, surface glossy and shining. At the aperture slightly contracted, mouth oval, flattened on one side. Septum much exserted, peaked on the curved side. As foreshortened to show the aperture in my drawing, the shell has a quaint resemblance to a tobacco pipe. Length 1·5; breadth ·64 mm.

Fig. 76.

Dredged at 36 fathoms N. 30° W. of Pava Islet and again at 150 fathoms off Beacon Islet (Funamanu).

The only species at all resembling this, figured in Tryon's Manual, is *C. nitidum*, Stimpson, than which it is less inflated.

TRIFORIS ASPERRIMUS, *Hinds.*
(Fig. 77.)

Hinds, Ann. Mag. Nat. Hist., xi., 1843, p. 18; Tryon, Man. Conch., ix., 1887, p. 181, pl. xxxviii., fig. 6.

A single, probably immature, specimen of twelve whorls, in length 2·92 and in breadth ·56 mm., which was dredged in 36 fathoms, north of Pava Islet is thus doubtfully determined. The species appears not to have been seen since Sir Edward Belcher dredged his unique specimen in eight fathoms on the Papuan coast.

Fig. 77.

MUREX RAMOSUS, *Linne.*

Tryon, Man. Conch., ii., 1880, p. 95, pl. i., figs. 1, 2.

A specimen was obtained by Mr. A. E. Finckh on one of the leeward islets of Funafuti.

CYPRÆA BECKI, *Gaskoin.*

Tryon, Man. Conch., vii., 1885, p. 91, pl. xvii., figs. 86, 87.

One specimen collected by Mr. W. Poole on the lagoon beach of Funafuti.

TURRICULA EXASPERATA, *Gmelin.*

Tryon, Man. Conch., iv., 1882, p. 180, pl. liii., figs. 541 – 544, pl. liv., figs. 545 – 546.

One dead shell dredged in 36 fathoms N. 30° W. of Pava Islet.

MARGINELLA ISSELI, *Nevill,* var. ELLICENSIS, *var. nov.*

(Fig. 78.)

Shell small, ovate, white, smooth, with a buried spire. Aperture narrow, crescentic. Outer lip arching from and above the vertex, thickened without and finely crenulate within, channeled anteriorly. Inner lip with a heavy layer of callus edged abruptly. Columella with three oblique entering folds, the posterior one small. Length 1·4; breadth ·64 mm.

Dredged at 36 fathoms north of Pava Islet, at 36 fathoms N. 30° W. of Pava Islet, and at 150 fathoms off Beacon Islet (Funamanu)

Fig. 78.

After much perplexity I have concluded not to separate this specifically from *M. isseli,* Nevill,[*] which agrees in size and shape but apparently differs by an additional fold on the columella. The example of that which Issel examined[†] had not the crenulated lip of the type. Savigny's work, containing the original description, is unfortunately inaccessible to me. No distinction is apparent to me between this species and *M. nympha,* Brazier,[‡] from Sydney Harbour.

Examples from Cape Sidmouth, Queensland, of what appears to be another variety of *M. isseli* are before me. They agree in shape but differ by being 2 mm. in length, and by having five plications on the columella.

[*] Tryon — Man. Conch., v., 1883, p. 40, pl. xi., fig. 39.
[†] Issel — Malac. del Mar Rosso, 1869, p. 117.
[‡] Brazier — Proc. Linn. Soc. N. S. W., (2) ix., 1894, p. 168, pl. xiv., fig. 2.

PTEROSOMA PLANA, *Lesson.*

Hedley, Proc. Malac. Soc., i., 1895, p. 333; Crosse, Journ. de Conch., xliv., 1896 (1897), pp. 207 - 212.

An imperfect shell from a depth of 200 fathoms off Tutaga Islet, is with doubt so identified. Since writing the article above quoted I have found that Fischer's reason for classing this as a Nemertine was a mistaken identification by the Naturalists of the "Challenger."*

ATLANTA GIBBOSA, *Eydoux and Souleyet.*

Eydoux and Souleyet, Voy. Bonite, Zool., ii., 1841, p. 386, pl. xxi., figs. 1 - 8.

Dead shells were dredged off Tutaga, in 45 – 52 and 200 fathoms. This species does not seem to have been recorded from the Pacific.

ATLANTA TURRICULATA, *D'Orbigny.*

Eydoux and Souleyet, *loc. cit.*, p. 391, pl. xxi., figs. 30 - 35.

Dredged off Tutaga Islet in 45 – 52 and 200 fathoms.

ATLANTA GUIDICHAUDII, *Eydoux and Souleyet.*

Eydoux and Souleyet, *loc. cit.*, p. 397, pl. xix., figs. 29 - 34.

Several dead shells dredged in 200 fathoms off Tutaga Islet.

TORNATINA LEPTEKES, *Watson.*

Pilsbry, Man. Conch., xv., 1893, p. 200, pl. xxiv., figs. 29, 30.

Dredged in 36 fathoms north of Pava Islet, and off Tutaga in 45 – 52 and 200 fathoms.

Previously taken off Raine Island, Queensland, by the "Challenger,"

RINGICULA, *sp.*

A small *Ringicula* was dredged in 45 – 52 fathoms off Tutaga Islet. It corresponds exactly to specimens from Torres Straits, which I have identified as *P. pusilla*, Watson, and differs very little from my *R. parvula*. It may be here pointed out that the illustration of *R. pusilla*,† appears to represent a young and broken shell, and that the description conveys a totally different idea of the species.

---

* Moseley—Ann. Mag. Nat. Hist., (4) xvi., 1875, p. 382.

† Watson—Chall. Rep., Zool., xv., 1886, pl. xlvii., fig. 9.

RINGICULA INCISA, *sp. nov.*

(Fig. 79.)

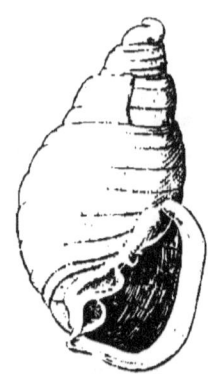

Fig. 79.

Shell ovate, glossy. Whorls five. Colour white. Sculpture—girt around the last whorl are eight nearly equidistant sharp furrows, sloping above and cut square below so as to carve the surface into descending steps. On the upper whorls there are three furrows. A distinct varix marks the penultimate whorl. Aperture ear-shaped, effuse and truncate anteriorly. Outer lip broadly reflected, rather straight, without tubercles. Inner lip with broad and strong plications below and a small one above. Length 2·2; breadth 1·2 mm.

One specimen dredged in 36 fathoms N. 30° W. of Pava Islet.

PHYLLIDIA VARICOSA, *Lamarck.*

Bergh, Reis. Archip. Philippinen, ii., 1876, p. 380, pl. lxxxvi., fig. 11.

Three specimens were collected by Mr. A. E. Finckh in the Funafuti lagoon.

CRYPTOPTHALMUS SMARAGDINUS, *Leuckart.*

Pilsbry, Man. Conch., xvi., 1895, p. 37, pl. vi., figs. 29 – 36.

Two specimens were taken by myself alive in shallow water in the lagoon. Mention of them was inadvertantly omitted from preceding pages. With them were taken an undetermined *Doris,* and an *Eolis.*

LIMACINA INFLATA, *D'Orbigny.*

H. and A. Adams, Genera Recent Mollusca, iii., 1858, pl. cxxxvii., figs. 2, 2a, 2b; Pelseneer, Chall. Rep., Zool., xxiii., 1888, p. 17.

Dead shells were dredged in abundance, off Tutaga Islet, in 45 – 52, 50 – 60, and 200 fathoms; in 36 fathoms north and in 36 fathoms N. 30° W. of Pava; and in 150 fathoms off Beacon Islet (Funamanu).

LIMACINA BULIMOIDES, *D'Orbigny.*

Rang and Souleyet, Hist. Nat. Pteropodes, 1852, p. 65, pl. xv., figs. 1 – 7; Pelseneer, *loc. cit.,* p. 30.

Dead shells dredged plentifully off Tutaga Islet in 36, 45 – 52 and 200 fathoms, and N. 30° W. of Pava Islet in 36 fathoms.

CLIO VIRGULA, *Rang.*

Rang and Souleyet, *loc. cit.,* p. 57, pl. vi., fig. 2, pl. xiii., figs. 20 – 24; Pelseneer, *loc. cit.,* p. 48.

A few shells dredged off Tutaga Islet in 45 – 52 and 200 fathoms and off Beacon Islet in 150 fathoms.

CLIO ACICULA, *Rang.*

Rang and Souleyet, *loc. cit.*, p. 56, pl. vi., figs. 5, 7; Pelseneer, *loc. cit.*, p. 51.

A few dead shells dredged in 200 fathoms off Tutaga Islet.

CLIO STRIATA, *Rang.*

Rang and Souleyet, *loc. cit.*, p. 55, pl. vi., fig. 3; Pelseneer, *loc. cit.*, p. 51.

One broken specimen from 45 – 52 fathoms off Tutaga Islet.

CLIO SUBULA, *Quoy and Gaimard.*

Rang and Souleyet, *loc. cit.*, p. 55, pl. vi., fig. 1; Pelseneer, *loc. cit.*, p. 57.

Numerous dead shells dredged off Tutaga Islet in 45 – 52 and 200 fathoms.

CLIO PYRAMIDATA, *Linne.*

Rang and Souleyet, *loc. cit.*, p. 50, pl. v., figs. 7 – 11; Pelseneer, *loc. cit.*, p. 63.

Dredged off Tutaga Islet in 45 – 52 and 200 fathoms.

CUVIERINA COLUMNELLA, *Rang.*

Boas, Spolia Atlantica, 1885, pl. iii., fig. 39; Pelseneer, *loc. cit.*, p. 67.

One specimen dredged in 200 fathoms off Tutaga Islet.

CAVOLINIA QUADRIDENTATA, *Lesueur.*

Boas, *loc. cit.*, p. 99, pl. i., fig. 4, pl. ii., fig. 15; Pelseneer, *loc. cit.*, p. 78.

A few dead specimens dredged off Tutaga Islet, in 45 – 52 and 200 fathoms.

CAVOLINIA LONGIROSTRIS, *Lesueur.*

Boas, *loc. cit.*, p. 102, pl. i., fig. 5, pl. ii., fig. 16; Pelseneer, *loc. cit.*, p. 79.

One dead specimen dredged in 200 fathoms off Tutaga Islet.

CAVOLINIA INFLEXA, *Lesueur.*

Boas, *loc. cit.*, p. 123, pl. i., fig. 11, pl. ii., fig. 21; Pelseneer, *loc. cit.*, p. 85.

Dredged off Tutaga Islet in 45 – 52 and 200 fathoms.

AGADINA STIMPSONI, *A. Adams.*

Pelseneer, *loc. cit.*, p. 31, pl. i., figs. 11 – 14.

A few specimens dredged off Tutaga Islet in 45 – 52 and 200 fathoms and north of Pava in 36 fathoms.

PELECYPODA.

ARCA PTEROESSA, *Smith.*

Smith, Chall. Rep., Zool., xiii., 1885, p. 262, pl. xvii., fig. 4.

Two small separate valves were dredged at 200 fathoms off Tutaga Islet.

ARCA CONGENITA, *Smith.*

Smith, *loc. cit.*, p. 264, pl. xvii., fig. 6.

One small valve from 50 - 60 fathoms off Tutaga Islet.

LIMOPSIS DAVIDIS, *sp. nov.*

(Fig. 80.)

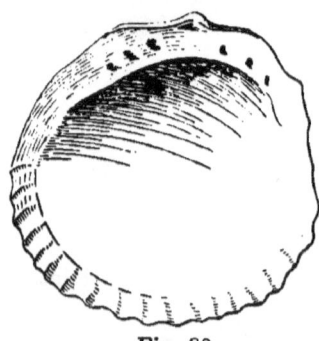

Shell small, suborbicular, flattened, scarcely inequilateral. Colour white, with a few, small, scattered brown dots. Posterior margin truncate; ventral and anterior margins rounded. Umbo prominent. Epidermis denuded. Sculpture—about twenty-four, prominent, radiating ridges sharply crenulate the margin and fade away before reaching the umbo, these are separated by flat interstices of about twice their breadth. They are more prominent and closer together at the posterio-ventral side, but for a space in the posterior slope one or two seem missing. The whole valve is covered with close concentric wrinkles, which become coarser as the ventral margin is approached. Hinge area very broad and rather curved, teeth three on each side. Internal margin crenulate. Height 1·22, length 1·22 mm.

One valve from 45 – 52 fathoms off Tutaga Islet.

Fig. 80.

Named in honour of Prof. T. W. E. David, B.A., under whose auspices it was secured.

If adult this species is the smallest known member of the genus In several respects it approaches *L. antillensis*, Dall,[*] which is deeper, and has certain internal tubercles absent in *L. davidi*.

LIMEA PECTINATA, *H. Adams*.

H. Adams, Proc. Zool. Soc., 1870, p. 7, pl. i., fig. 11.

One valve from 36 fathoms N. 30° W. of Pava.

This is the first appearance of either species or genus in the Pacific.

PECTEN SPECIOSUS, *Reeve*.

Reeve, Conch. Icon., viii., pl. xxvii., sp. 112.

One living example was taken in the lagoon by Mr. A. E. Finckh.

CRASSATELLA *sp.*

A fragment of a *Crassatella* which might belong to *C. rhomboides*, Smith, was taken off Tutaga in 50 – 60 fathoms.

ADDENDA.—Since revising the preceding pages, I have found among the shells which I collected at Funafuti, the following additional species :—*Engina lineata*, Reeve; *Sistrum dumosum*, Conrad; and *Sistrum undatum*, Chemnitz.

---

[*] Dall—Bull. Mus. Comp. Zool., xii., 1886, p. 237, pl. viii., fig. 7.

www.ingramcontent.com/pod-product-compliance
Lightning Source LLC
Chambersburg PA
CBHW030901050726
47500CB00009B/808